RICHARD HOLLOWAY

Anger
Sex
Doubt
&
Death

First published in Great Britain 1992
SPCK
Holy Trinity Church
Marylebone Road
London NW1 4DU

Acknowledgement

The author is grateful to John Murray (Publishers) Ltd
for permission to reproduce John Betjeman's poem
'Old Friends' from *High and Low*, first published in 1966.

British Library Cataloguing-in-Publication Data

CIP data for this book is available from the British Library

ISBN 0-281-04616-6

Typeset by Pioneer Associates, Perthshire, Scotland
Printed and bound in Great Britain by
BPCC Hazells Ltd
Member of BPCC Ltd

For
Nadir Dinshaw

Contents

Preface

Anger, Sex, Doubt and Death. When I began to write on sources of stress in the life of Christian ministers I quickly identified these as the four areas of greatest difficulty.

Originally, in writing about Anger, I had intended to deal with the experience of human anger but, as often happens in a piece of writing, the theme asserted itself in a way different from my intention. I found myself addressing, in a particular way, the theme of divine anger in Christianity, as expressed in the doctrine of damnation, and I soon realized that the anger was mine, anger at what I considered to be the ugly and sadistic subtext of classical Christianity. The anger shows in the text. I have done little to neutralize it. I hope it is balanced by the underlying theme of the book, which is my increasing conviction that the Christian gospel, beneath the moralistic accretions that have characterized it, is about the unconditional grace and forgiveness of God.

The chapters on Sex, Doubt and Death are more straightforwardly and obviously about sources of stress for the Christian minister, both personally and professionally. Unhealthy attitudes to sexuality continue to disfigure the Christian community. Doubt accompanies faith, but it is not always a companion welcome to the Christian. Death, the last enemy, is a reality we must all deal with. This book reflects one man's thinking on all these topics.

I have added an epilogue on the central claim of the gospel, why it is *good* news, why it invites the response of gratitude rather than fear. The Decade of Evangelism has become another stress-point for generous-minded Christians. This is because increasingly vocal groups in our society have made Christianity into, not a gospel of grace, but yet another religious ideology engaged in a power struggle for a bigger market share. If we really understood the gospel within the gospel we would not be able to resist sharing it, but it would be out of joy, not from religious superiority.

This book is based on lectures I gave in 1991 at the invitation of members of the Faculty of Theology at Durham University. I am grateful to them for giving me the opportunity to muse on these topics, and to Christine Roy, my secretary, for her help in preparing the text for publication.

Richard Holloway
Edinburgh, January 1992

Anger

Is the Christian message good news for sinners? That
is the question. By sinners I mean *sinners*, not reformed
sinners or sinners who have just repented, but real
sinners, practising sinners, who are either helpless or
defiant. It claims to be, but historically the claim doesn't
stand up. The essence of the historic attitude is
captured very well in Shakespeare's *Hamlet*, where
Hamlet finds his hated stepfather at prayer and decides
to kill him:

> Now might I do it pat, now he is praying;
> And now I'll do't: — and so he goes to heaven;
> And so am I reveng'd: — that would be scanned:
> A villain kills my father; and, for that,
> I his sole son, do this same villain send
> To heaven.
> O, this is hire and salary, not revenge.
> He took my father grossly, full of bread;
> With all his crimes broad blown, as flush as May;
> And how his audit stands who knows save heaven?
> But, in our circumstance and course of thought,
> 'Tis heavy with him: and am I, then, revenged,
> To take him in the purging of his soul,

1

When he is fit and season'd for his passage?
No.
Up, sword; and know thou a more horrid hent:
When he is drunk asleep, or in his rage;
Or in th' incestuous pleasure of his bed;
At gaming, swearing; or about some act
That has no relish of salvation in't; —
Then trip him, that his heels may kick at heaven;
And that his soul may be as damn'd and black
As hell, whereto it goes.[1]

There's much beauty and urgency in that approach, a dramatic finality to it. My own mind's eye captures in imagination millions of battlefield deaths, as despairing sinners cry out to someone, 'Confess me, confess me. Shrive me, shrive me. Don't let me go to God with my sins unpurged. Shrive me now so that when I breathe my last I won't go to hell.' There is also the sinner's heroism, expressed by the defiant ones who refuse to repent, refuse cravenly to crawl on their bellies to God at the last. 'Thus have I lived, thus will I die. I enjoyed my sins. They brought me pleasure, and I will not repudiate them now. I am loyal to my follies. I refuse to betray them for fear of this heavenly tyrant. Lead me to hell.' T. S. Eliot would probably describe that as doing the wrong thing for the right reason, knowing that the greatest treason is to do the right thing for the wrong reason.

So let's look at this message of good cheer Christians are supposed to stand for. Evangelists we call ourselves, bearers of glad tidings, heralds of good news. To the men and women of the earth, with its complicated history of joy and sorrow, is it good news we bring them? Have they thought it was good news in the past? Well it depends how you look at it. If you've ever seen the *Dirty Harry* films of Clint Eastwood, you'll recognize the endlessly repeated scene where he points his massive handgun in some villain's face and says, 'If you stop annoying me I won't blow your head off, but since I enjoy blowing heads off, make my day, go for it!' There are various 'make my day' versions of Christianity, certainly in popular understanding as reflected in literature and art. In the film of the life of Christy Brown, *My Left Foot*, there is one scene that captures this side of Christianity perfectly. Christy Brown was the Irish poet, artist and novelist, who suffered from cerebral palsy and typed his stories and his poetry and painted his pictures with his left foot. There is one scene in the film where he is being instructed in the faith by his parish priest. The priest tells him that the souls of the departed can get out of purgatory and we can help them by praying for them and lighting candles but, he says fiercely, they can never ever get out of hell. And you see the stark, twisted, frightened face of the little boy listening to this sadistic teaching, his eyes like saucers. There's a well-known South American evangelist who, in his addresses at evangelical rallies, tells his hearers that he knows his grandfather is in hell, because he didn't give his life to Christ. We can get out of purgatory but we can never, ever get out of hell.

Hell-fire versions of salvation have a simple logic. They are, in all their versions, reward religions, doctrines of salvation by works, even though the work may only be the last muttered act of contrition before the light dies. As such, they are easy to understand and very easy to explain. You describe the kind of conduct that gets people into hell and the kind that gets them into heaven, and tell them to take their pick. The old moral theologians in the Catholic tradition had this very carefully graded and worked out. All sins were punished, but not all sins were punished eternally. There were venial sins that got you an indeterminate sentence in purgatory, but you could, as we have already seen, get out of purgatory. You did your sentence, aided by the prayers of your friends still alive, and you made it after a period of purgatorial rehabilitation into the nearer presence of God. Other sins, however, were mortal. They damned you for ever. There was no rehabilitation programme for such sins, though there was always this magical mystical grasp at salvation by the final act of contrition, hence the drama of one's own death: a fearful thing it was to die suddenly and unprepared, 'unhouseled and unaneled', unabsolved and unanointed, as Shakespeare puts it. The agents of that ultimate salvation were the clergy, who heard those last confessions and issued those final passports. One only has to say that to recognize the enormous power that was made to reside in these men.* There is a splendour and drama about it all, which is why it lends itself to great narrative and tragedy.

*Though it is only fair to add that, as with the sacrament of baptism, lay people could administer the rites *in articulo mortis* in the absence of a priest.

Not all versions of 'make my day' Christianity are so logical. There are, for instance, the extraordinary predestination theories, which sound like sketches from Monty Python, in which arbitrariness is raised to a state beyond lunacy. One can almost hear John Cleese setting the sketch up. '*Right*, this is God here. I want all you people to get into groups of 500. I've decided to save two out of each group — so line up! Right, now! You there, in the front row, step forward; you there, in the back row, step back! Right! The rest of you turn left and walk into that large gas oven over there.'

The arbitrariness of predestination is captured scathingly by Robert Burns in his famous poem, 'Holy Willie's Prayer':

> O thou that in the Heavens does dwell,
> Wha, as it pleases best Thysel,
> Sends ane to Heaven an' ten to Hell
>   A' for thy glory,
> And no for onie gude or ill
>   They've done before Thee![2]

Is that kind of thing good news even for the saved? Would you want to get close to that kind of God, even if he did tell you he'd predestined you to salvation, while everyone else in your neighbourhood was going to hell? How could you be sure that he hadn't got worse games in store for you on the other side? If it were proved beyond doubt that that is the kind of God we have, and that that indeed is the kind of fate that awaits most of God's children, I would be tempted to return the ticket, like Ivan Karamazov, in Dostoevsky's great novel, who simply refuses to play the religious game any longer, because nothing in the wide universe can justify the torture of a single child.

Another version of predestination, though not quite so arbitrary, is what we might call semantic salvation, or salvation by formula. Here the criterion that determines our eternal destination is not so much moral as epistemological. Even the virtuous are damned, unless they have come to what is called a saving knowledge of Jesus Christ. The best that St Augustine could negotiate for virtuous pagans or young children who died unbaptized, was a sort of shadowy existence in the *limbo puerorum*, a state best described as an everlasting case of post-viral depression spent sitting in an underground shelter, waiting for an 'all clear' that never comes. Again the arbitrariness of it irresistibly suggests a John Cleese sketch: a soul arrives at the gate of heaven and knocks: 'Please, let me in. I've come home.' 'You can't get in here, unless you know the password.' 'But no one told me the password.' 'I know.' 'Well, then, it can't be my fault — so let me in.' 'You can't get in unless you know the password.'

'Caricature', you may say, but caricature artistically heightens the distinctive features in a personality or a face, and these caricatures of Christianity certainly capture what has been one of its most powerful characteristics. Today it may be seen at its cleanest and clearest only in reactionary sects on the far right, but it creates an atmosphere and has defined a tradition that is anything but good news for sinners. It is quite the opposite, it is very bad news indeed for the world of confused humanity, as it struggles with its own fears and longings. Some feminist theologians today say Christianity is intrinsically and incurably patriarchal and sexist, and call upon women to leave it to its own devices and move out into a freer, less pathological religious position. It would be equally legitimate, I believe, to describe Christianity as being almost intrinsically and incurably cruel and hateful, with its angry God and his final solution to the problem of sinners, those messy, intractable creatures that God himself called into existence.

The theological paradigm behind this phenomenon is the ancient debate between faith and works. Is humanity saved by grace through faith, and is it therefore able to achieve works of righteousness? Or is salvation achieved through works of righteousness that demonstrate the existence of saving faith? Both emphases are found in the New Testament. The debate is not just between the letters of Paul and the letter of James, but within Paul himself. It is an unresolved debate that runs right through Scripture. It can be read back into the Gospels and the words of Jesus, especially into the parables. It is not a debate or a tension that the New Testament itself resolves for us, though doubtless we would all claim a New Testament basis for our particular resolution of the conflict. For instance, there are parables that unforgettably proclaim the unconditional love of God, such as the parable of the prodigal son, and the parable of the labourers in the vineyard; but there are other parables, such as the parable of Dives and Lazarus, the poor man who lay at his gate, and the parable of final judgement in Matthew 25, that tell a different story.

But it is in Paul that we see the tension between these two theological poles at its most extreme. Paul described himself as the worst of sinners. He is the poet of penitence and the celebrant of mercy, proclaiming his revolutionary doctrine of justification by faith alone. One senses in his almost incoherent proclamation of this great doctrine an impossible attempt to find verbal equivalents for a mystical insight of revolutionary immediacy, so he is led to develop metaphors to describe it, such as the metaphor of justification, except that in this court the guilty are proclaimed innocent; or the metaphor of redemption, in which slaves with no rights and no funds are redeemed, bought out, by the generosity of God. But Paul, the spiritual genius who first penetrated to the heart of Christ's revelation of the nature of God, was also and more than residually, Paul the Pharisee, Paul the moralist, Paul the conservative Roman citizen, made afraid by his knowledge of the explosive human potential for licence and disorder. So the poet of justification by faith through the unmerited grace of God, becomes the rigorist who excommunicates sinners and announces that idolaters and adulterers will never gain access to the kingdom Christ died to bequeath them.

I know that Christian theologians have satisfied themselves that they have integrated these mutually contradictory theological truths. There have been several approaches to this problem, the most severe probably reflected in the Johanine Epistles. Here the good news is that all sin before baptism is forgivable; the bad news, that post-baptismal sin is not forgivable. This resolution of the problem gave rise to the quaint, understandable, but risky tradition of deathbed conversion. Timed accurately, one could enjoy a life of sinful pleasure; and just before death, when sin, anyway, had probably lost its allure, one could call for the palace chaplain or the local bishop, confess one's sins, be baptized and issued into eternal bliss.

This doctrine appeared too rigorous and unkind to succeeding generations who discovered that post-baptismal sin was the rule rather than the exception, so there developed the discipline of confession. Tertullian called this the second plank after shipwreck. We were shipwrecked by our sin and baptism was the first plank thrown to us. When we went under again, confession was the second plank that was tossed to us. It had three parts. First of all, there had to be genuine contrition, genuine sorrow for sins committed against God's love; then there had to be confession of the sin committed. This was not a quiet, discreet little whisper to a priest in a corner. It was public confession to the bishop in the presence of the church, for sin was an offence against the whole family; it was not just a private matter. After confession there followed satisfaction, which might involve the restitution of something that had been stolen, for instance, though it could go much further than this to include a programme of amendment of life that gave evidence of change and repentance. If this satisfaction was shown over a period, sometimes over years, the bishop

9

would formally pronounce absolution and the sinner would be restored to communion and full fellowship with the church.

However, the Christian Church, even at its most rigorous, has always found ways of tempering the wind to the shorn lamb, so the appealing psychodrama of public confession gradually gave way to private confession, though hanging over the whole matter there was still the threat of eternal damnation. That was how the Church handled this uncomfortable dualism in its institutional practice; but that is not the same thing as coming to a genuine theological resolution. In order to achieve that, theologians have resorted to a kind of word-game approach that is perilously close to hypocrisy. We *are* redeemed, they tell us, saved, rescued from destruction, by the unmerited grace of God. That is the bottom line, that is the good news. We are not saved by our works, our morality, our good behaviour. On the other hand, if we are truly saved and have heard and processed the news of this amazing fact, it will result in our transformation, our sanctification. The evidence that we have genuinely heard the good news will lie in our subsequent behaviour.

Further subtleties emerge. The redeemed show forth the fruits of redemption in their conduct; the implication being, and sometimes it is spelled out explicitly, that if you don't show the fruits of redemption in your life, you obviously can't be redeemed. However, one development, called antinomianism, went in the opposite direction. It had a very appealing logic. If we have already been saved, predestined to eternal salvation by the love of God, then we can behave as we like. There are echoes of this position in Paul's letters. He struggles with the logic of salvation and resolves the dilemma posed by his own insights by having his cake and refusing to eat it. We are saved by grace, but it's wrong to sin in order to make grace more abundant. Here the poet and the apostle, the mystic and the bishop wrestle together, and it's the lawyer that wins, the institutional logic that prevails.

Speaking personally, I find that neither the New Testament nor the subsequent history of the Church has really resolved the dilemma to my satisfaction, either as a student or, more importantly, as a sinner. Increasingly, I think the dilemma isn't really a dilemma at all. I don't think we are presented with apparently contradictory truths, or antinomies. I don't believe that this is a foundational Christian paradox of the same sort as the christological paradoxes that celebrate the humanity and the divinity of Christ or the unity and trinity of the godhead. I think the real edge in this dispute about grace and works is on a different level. The first question is 'How am I saved?', and the answer to that is good news. I am saved by the unconditional mercy of God, through Christ, who died for me while I was yet in my sins. The next question is 'How can I become a good, or even just a better human being?' That is an important but separate question, which has been fatefully linked to the salvation question. It accounts for the incoherence and internal confusion of much theology, especially in the Western tradition, with its built-in Pelagian bias. Faith and morality, though they may be related, are different and one does not depend upon the other. We are either saved by grace and can celebrate the fact, leaving the problem of our behaviour to a separate department, while duly acknowledging its importance; or we are not, we are saved by our works, our morality, our good behaviour. In spite of the historic attempts at linkage, we can't have it both ways. Morality is either superior or subsidiary to grace.

Most people get in a dither when confronted by this challenge, especially if, like the British, they have a fear of chaos and a passion for order. The British like their faith systems to support morality and national stability. This was something that was acutely perceived by the nobleman in Rebecca West's novel *The Birds Fall Down*:

> . . . the piety of the English is a mockery. They want a prescription for social order and union with God means nothing to them. So they pretend that this is what religion is for: to teach men and women to be moral. But we Russians know that religion is for the moral and the immoral. It is the love of God for man meeting with the love of man for God, and God loves the vicious and the criminal and the idle as well as He loves the industrious and the honest and the truthful and the abstinent. He humbles himself to ask for the love of the murderer, the drunkard, the liar, the beggar, the thief. Only God can achieve this sublime and insane relationship.[3]

Russian mystical irrationalism increasingly appeals to me, because I am tired of the smallness and narrowness, the pettiness, the need to hate and persecute, in moralistic Christianity. I don't find that in Christ. In him I find an enormous passion for holiness and generosity of spirit, allied to a profound loathing for hypocrisy. The paradox is, of course, that Christ's acceptance of me in my sinfulness is more likely to woo me out of my sins than the hectoring moralizers who only confirm me in my self-disgust and make me run for cover.

There is a question here we must all decide, because it will have profound effects upon our attitude to many things. It will clearly affect our attitude towards our own sinfulness, but more important will be its effect on our attitude towards other sinners, especially towards those whose sins we fear. We know more about the psychological complexities of human conduct than we used to. We understand something about the mechanism of projection, the fear that turns us into persecutors, the self-doubt that turns us into inquisitors, so a lot will depend on the size of our God. To go back to the original problem: God either declares the guilty innocent, forgives them, reprieves them time after time; or he punishes the guilty and rewards the innocent, maybe even in this life, though with no obvious system, but certainly and devastatingly in the world to come. We are either saved by God's mercy or we procure our salvation or damnation by our own efforts.

Is the Christian message good news for sinners, or bad news, then? Is it a vision of God's unconditional love or a moral crusade? That's the question I asked at the beginning. It's still our question. There's no doubt how the person on the Clapham omnibus would

13

answer. Western Christianity has been relentlessly moralistic for centuries. That's certainly what the general perception is. It is one reason why whole sections of society believe they are constitutionally incapable of church membership, because they define themselves as inhabiting a culture of sin. They drink, they smoke, they gamble, they fornicate, they fiddle their taxes and steal from their work place, they don't work very hard, they take it easy, go easy, are of easy virtue. They don't feel comfortable in church, either socially or morally. They do not feel good enough. It's an extraordinary reversal this, because these were precisely the people who hung around Jesus, the publicans and sinners who didn't think they were good enough, and weren't, for the established religion of their day.

One of the most depressing things about being a Christian minister is the lowering effect we have on natural human conviviality, especially in its coarser expressions. It's not surprising that some ministers freeze all over and become what they're expected to be, while others try desperately to be 'unholier than thou'. What ministers are in danger of losing is that human naturalness that is uncomplicatedly good-natured and unhaunted by moralistic pressures, particularly of the meaner sort. It is not a question of the kind of behaviour we think is right. Appropriate human behaviour is obviously fundamental to human happiness and flourishing. It is not even a denial of the conviction that happiness and holiness are consubstantial, that the sinful cannot achieve happiness or psychological contentment as long as they are rubbing against the grain of the universe. The issue is *salvation*, everlasting access to the love of God. The question is, Do sinners have that while they are yet sinners, while they are in their sins, as one part of Scripture certainly teaches?

> While we were still weak, at the right time Christ died for the ungodly. Why, one will hardly die for a righteous man — though perhaps for a good man one will dare even to die. But God shows his love for us in that while we were yet sinners Christ died for us. Since, therefore, we are now justified by his blood, much more shall we be saved by him from the wrath of God. For if while we were enemies we were reconciled to God by the death of his Son, much more, now that we are reconciled, shall we be saved by his life. Not only so, but we also rejoice in God through our Lord Jesus Christ, through whom we have now received our reconciliation.
>
> (Romans 5.6-11)

Another way to come at the question is to ask what kind of God we believe in? It would be easy to get from certain themes in Scripture a picture of an angry God who is constantly irritated by the children he has created. He is a God who intricately programmes his children with sexuality, but seems to hate sex. He is a God who is elusive and ungraspable in his essence or actions, but appears to demand total faith in his own existence. He is a God who brings all to death, but appears to claim only some of them from everlasting night or everlasting torment. If this is our God, then our message is not good news. It may be urgent or important news, news we should share with others. There is no doubt at all that much of the Church's evangelistic urgency down the centuries has been fuelled by a passionate desire to rescue God's children from God's anger, either by making them submit to a sort of magical initiation or by radically reforming their conduct, so that their temporal vices will not be paid for at eternal prices. This may be important news to hear, but it isn't good news. It's like telling the chronically sick to get well, because sickness is a punishable offence.

I don't find that good news. I am increasingly repelled by anger, particularly divine anger. I am tired of angry voices and clenched fists. I am tired of all those crowds we watch on the television news, cursing their enemies, inflamed by their own self-righteousness. And I am tired of my own anger, my irritation at frustrations to my own plans, my resistance to criticism, my defensiveness, my fear of being found out, revealed as a phoney and a spiritual fraud. The virtue I increasingly treasure and covet for myself is kindness, even kindness towards the brutal, because most of us are victims before we are oppressors. Increasingly, this angry God seems like a brutal and brutalizing father of the sort we are all too familiar with in modern cases of child abuse, hitting out at his disordered offspring, exploiting and suppressing his womenfolk, handing out reward and punishment with a tormenting arbitrariness. We know a grèat deal about dysfunctional families nowadays. We know that dysfunctional families are created by dysfunctional parents, who were themselves created by dysfunctional parents, and so on *ad infinitum*. If the human race is a dysfunctional family, who parented it? Where has all that anger, including all that angry sex, come from?

We also know more about sexuality today. We may be no better at controlling or humanizing it, but we do understand how fragile and complex it is, and how mysteriously prone to disorder and disease. Even those who pride themselves on their sexual straightforwardness are aware that their sexuality is a baffling mixture of an almost ungovernable biological urge and a mysterious need for connection and surrender that is never permanently satisfied and is therefore constantly pursued.

And we live in a society in which, though we long for it, faith is much more difficult to find, especially if we are not prepared to park our minds outside church before going in.

Finally, we are afraid to die, or rather, we are so passionately fond of life that leaving it fills us with sorrow, just as the death of our friends fills us with grief.

This, then, is my condition. I am afraid of an angry God and afraid of my own anger, and find nothing noble in either. I am filled with sexual longings that I cannot always control. I long for faith but am racked by doubt. And I am sickened by dying, especially the dying of the young or the cutting down of people in the full maturity of their lives, as well as of the meanness and misery that often accompanies the dying of the aged. That is where I am. If the Christian message is good news for me, it must be good news for me there in that place, in my anger, in my lust, in my doubt and in my dying. It must meet me there and be good news for me there, because that, I suspect, is where I shall remain. And I believe it *is* good news for me there, but not as it has been received or preached by some Christian evangelists. I believe that before we can tackle the problem presented to our humanity by morality and mortality, we must first establish the basis of our salvation, the good news of God made known in Christ. We need to do this not only for our own sake but for the sake of those to whom we are sent, before whom we shall preach and to whom we shall minister. We need to reclaim the knowledge that, as Dean Inge put it, 'Christianity is good news, not good advice'.

We have to separate salvation from sanctification. Scripture does not obviously do this, but Scripture is not a systematic treatise. Scripture is like a vast archaeological site which we reconstruct by intelligent guesswork and inspiration, and we need a principle of interpretation that will help us to evaluate what we find. I would like to suggest a principle called 'dynamic personal continuity', which is based on a living if elusive relationship with the mystery of God. Responding to that relationship is not an exact science, but a type of trust that gives us the confidence to risk, to experiment and even to fail. Behind that creative and untidy response there lies confidence in the love of the God who loves us first. We know enough about human security to recognize that good parents, by their steady love of their children, endow them with a security that enables them to take risks and live creatively, without looking over their shoulders endlessly for parental approval. Many people have been programmed by their early years to fear failure. They constantly need approval from grudging parents. They have been formed into the mould of the authoritarian personality, who has more fear of failure than hope for success. Another characteristic of this type of personality is its need to obey without explanation. People like this live their lives reactively, they are always responding to a threatening inner stimulus. They cannot live proactively, adventurously, they find it difficult to engage with the future.

The religious parallels are clear and obvious. If our God is an authoritarian idol, whose approval we earn by good deeds and works of righteousness, a God who will accept us only if we obey the rules, then we shall turn into moralistic, unadventurous, uncreative creatures, whose very virtues are bred of fear and conformity. But if our God is the one who loves us from all eternity, dying for us in our sins, the one whom we love because he loves us first, then we are given an enormous inner security or confidence that enables us to make our lives a loving adventure. Adult children of loving parents, though they wander far from them in their own pilgrimage, have interiorized their love and carry it with them to the end. This was one of Bonhoeffer's great insights and it enabled him to make the ambiguous decisions he had to make in a messy, fallen but ultimately redeemed universe. We make our choices boldly, because our confidence, he wrote, 'depends on a God who demands responsible action in a bold venture of faith and who promises forgiveness and consolation to the man who becomes a sinner in that venture.'[4]

The courage to live like that, the courage to risk and create, to take chances and make mistakes, comes from the original security of endowed love. Reinhold Niebuhr recognized this fact in one of his later books:

> . . . the capacity of the self to relate itself to others cannot be achieved by a robust moral will. It is a gift of the original security of grace.
>
> Erich Fromm in his *Man for Himself* defines the capacity to love as a 'phenomenon of abundance', but mistakenly he assumes that the abundance of security which enables the self to love is derived from its previous self-seeking. It is more correct to regard the abundance of security as furnished by the love and devotion which others give the self, as Erik Erikson, for example, illustrates with his concept of 'basic trust'. Thus we have a complete circle of the paradox: consistent self-seeking is self-defeating; but self-giving is impossible to the self without resources furnished by the community, in the first instance, the family.[5]

The pure essence of the Christian message is that God loves us everlastingly, unconditionally. This love is our salvation, our original security. We were first loved, therefore we can love. 'We love, because he first loved us' (1 John 4.19). That is the good news. In your very sin you are loved. Obviously not *for* your sin, but even *in* your sin. It is that acceptance that gives us the assurance on which all moral behaviour is built. We know that in ordering human societies we cannot wait for the slow, incremental work of sanctification to take place. Human societies have to be based on law, the assumption of the fallenness of humanity. It may be that the Church, as a human institution in history, has to model itself on law and discipline, as well. Nevertheless, this necessity is a decline from the original sublimity of pure grace. Inasmuch as the Church, as a social unit, exercises discipline and restraint, it reflects the nature of the world that dare not base its dealings on love, but on wariness and self-interest. This is why, though the Church is in some sense a foretaste of salvation, it is not a true bearer of it, even though, from time to time in its history, it produces saints whose acceptance of sinners is Godlike in its absoluteness and extremity.

Few of us achieve this level of acceptance. Most of us model our idea of the Church on the societies of earth rather than on the society of heaven. This is an unavoidable, though tragic necessity; but it becomes doubly tragic if we fail to recognize what we are doing. Sanctity is never the result of obeying the law that is based on a system of reward and punishment. Sanctity is always based on the conviction that goodness is its own good and partakes of the nature of God. It can only happen at all on the basis of absolute assurance of grace.

As we have noticed, the tragedy of disturbed and dysfunctional children is that they have no original endowment of love from which to grow. We, too, are dysfunctional children, if we have not learnt in the

very depths of our heart that our salvation has already
been secured, that we are safe. This is a psychological
as well as a theological need. Of course, it raises many
unanswerable questions about the consequences, for
instance, of unrepented sin. To deal with that question
in an aside is imprudent, but it seems to me that the
clue lies in understanding that, in the universe of our
kind of God, sooner or later it is likely to dawn on us
that we are loved, wherever we are, an insight captured
in Edwin Muir's poem 'Transfiguration', where he sees
the whole story of the fall of humanity recapitulated
and undone.

> But he will come again, it's said, though not
> Unwanted and unsummoned; for all things,
> Beasts of the field, and woods, and rocks, and seas,
> And all mankind from end to end of the earth
> Will call him with one voice. In our own time,
> Some say, or at a time when time is ripe.
> Then he will come, Christ the uncrucified,
> Christ the discrucified, his death undone,
> His agony unmade, his cross dismantled
> — Glad to be so — and the tormented wood
> Will cure its hurt and grow into a tree
> In a green springing corner of young Eden,
> And Judas damned take his long journey backward
> From darkness into light and be a child
> Beside his mother's knee, and the betrayal
> Be quite undone and never more be done.[6]

But this is an unnecessary avenue to explore. The
gospel of the love of God is not meant to raise abstract
questions about others but existential questions about

ourselves. It is addressed quite personally to each of us. Our Lord's words to Peter are the best wisdom when we are tempted to speculate on the destiny of others, 'What is that to thee? follow thou me' (John 21.22). It is true that the existence of evil men and women creates problems for us, but we also know about the circularity, the repetitiveness, as well as the banality of evil:

> In the lost boyhood of Judas
> Christ was betrayed.[7]

This may be the clue to the mystery of anger. There may be a righteous anger, as theologians have alleged, which is the other side of God's love, God's loving impatience with our follies. There may be as much in that approach as theologians have argued, but even here I think we ought to be careful. In human beings even righteous anger is likely to be something else as well. Human beings are prone to victimizing. They project their fears and fantasies onto scapegoats, who are punished, not for their own sins, but for the sins of their tormentors. The paradigm of this complicated human response is the fate of sexual offenders in prison, who become ritual victims for the other inmates. It may be that the pure in heart are capable of a righteous anger that is absolutely on behalf of others and is a proper desire to redress the balance of injustice against the poor and the weak, but it is almost impossible for us to avoid self-righteousness here. The anger I know best is my own and it is rarely righteous. The usual arena for anger is the family. It invariably has to do with frustration and lack of self-control, with the impatience that is the refusal to endure or suffer discomfort. Within each of us is a sensitive core of frustration — press it and we get angry. My anger can be triggered by someone else's excessive noise; by someone's refusal to see my point of view; by anything that presses against my own projects, my own carefully organized comfort, whether it is physical, spiritual or intellectual. Press against any of these and you'll get my adrenaline flowing. We know how much anger there is in families. We know the terrible consequences in spouse and child abuse, sexual, physical, mental. And behind it lies this raw, twisted, unlovely and unloved human ego, screaming in its own pain and self-hatred, striking out at the very thing it loves.

Though the family is the commonest scene and source of anger, the Church is another focus. So is the ministry of the Church. There are lots of angry people around. Sometimes anger is a kind of displacement, a sort of referred psychic pain. Ministers are sometimes baffled by the anger they occasion in others. It can take a great deal of patience to discover that the anger is usually aimed at something they represent and not at them, though they make convenient targets, places to which the painful anger can be referred. Sooner or later people in authority come up against this phenomenon, what the American military would call 'an attitude problem'. It takes long and loving patience to work through it and few of us are equipped with that. But there are human reflections of the divine patience. I have watched my own daughter work with mentally handicapped children and marvelled at her strength and patience, as she has stayed with them through their rages, bearing their bruises, never raising her voice, the very paradigm of the divine love.

Sometimes anger is a group thing. It can be a rejection of reality and necessity as represented by the other, the thing from outside, whether it's another race, another nation, another gender, another point of view. It is perceived as an invasion of our territory, a threat to our balance and equanimity, so we reach metaphorically or actually for the gun above the driving mirror. Sometimes anger seems to be bred of intellectual laziness, the laziness that cannot be bothered to respond to a new truth, an impending reality, the insistent pressure of change. And there is anger at time itself. This kind of anger is a tragic but understandable rejection of reality, its pains and frustrations. Like a clumsy and impatient child playing with unco-operative building blocks, frustrated by its own ineptitude, we knock over what we have half built and blame the universe for our anger, so unlike the infinite patience of God.

Each of these types of anger points to an opposing strategy for human beings. Know yourself inwardly, understand your wounds. Know whom you hate and why. Engage with the real world and not some idealized version of it. Engage with the real Church and with its actual history. One of the most unattractive of human types is the angry nostalgic or romantic, who sneeringly berates the leaders of changing institutions and blames them for their own pain at time's onward rush. Do not make a virtue, especially a spiritual virtue, out of your own inertia or desire to be left in peace, or even out of your angry desire to kick up a storm.

Know your type, your tendency, who you are. Don't be so sure that God is made in your image exclusively.

Some years ago Bishop John Robinson in the Saturday religious slot in *The Times* wrote a piece called 'Is God Right or Left Wing?' He pointed out that a cogent case could be made for either claim. A case could be made out for other things besides, but God is bigger than our partial vision. That is why we should remember that we are loved even in our anger. We may scream and rage in our loneliness and pain; 'underneath are the everlasting arms'.

Notes

1 William Shakespeare, *Hamlet*, III.iii.78.
2 Robert Burns, 'Holy Willie's Prayer'.
3 Rebecca West, *The Birds Fall Down*. Macmillan 1966.
4 Dietrich Bonhoeffer, *Letters and Papers from Prison* (Longmans, Green & Co. 1944), p. 63.
5 Reinhold Niebuhr, *Man's Nature and His Communities* (Scribner & Son 1965), pp. 108ff.
6 Edwin Muir, 'Transfiguration'. In *Collected Poems*. Faber & Faber 1964.
7 George Russell (AE), quoted in Norman Sherry, *The Life of Graham Greene*, vol. 1 (Penguin 1989), p. 91.

If our salvation is assured how, then, do we deal with sex? This question is usually put the other way round. How do I deal with my sexuality so that it will not damn me? This has rendered sexuality perilous. It stretches like a quivering tightrope across a bottomless abyss. One slip and we fall headlong into the pit. It is not surprising, therefore, that such a perilous pursuit has become overloaded with significance, both by those who espouse the Christian ethic and by those who eschew it. How can we handle wisely and talk sanely about something as complex as sexuality if we treat it so momentously? However, if we defuse it, remove something of its momentousness, it may help us to act wisely.

The momentousness of sexuality has been interpreted differently in different cultures. In Christianity we have inherited a pollution theory of sexuality that probably made sense in its original context, but has become meaningless today. Nevertheless, it has provided a series of powerfully negative metaphors for sexuality that still haunt us. In one of my parishes I had two parishioners who had met and married while they were both long-term patients in a mental hospital.

They were released into the community and did very well, on the whole. One day he came to me and told me of his distress because the marriage had never been consummated. When I spoke to her about the matter she giggled and said she'd 'huv nane o' that fulth'. She was fond of her whisky and I suggested that an extra dose that night might make all the difference to their marriage, and so it proved. In her untutored way she was reflecting the 'dirt' theory of sex that is surprisingly persistent. Yeats caught the confusion perfectly when he wrote, 'Love has pitched his mansion in the place of excrement.'[1] Dirt has been defined as 'matter out of place'. On one level it is a straightforward concept: jam in the pot or on one's morning toast is jam, but splattered on the table, or sticking to one's jacket, it is dirt; it is jam out of place. Our vital fluids, though they have their place, are messy. Semen, saliva and menstrual fluid can become dirt, in this objective sense of matter out of place. Once the idea of dirt becomes a metaphor that is potently internalized, it becomes loaded with a dangerous meaning.

For some reason sexuality as dirt has become transferred to our culture from the Old Testament, while dietary dirt has not, though it is part of the same phenomenon. Just as the Levitical code pronounced certain vital fluids to be dirt or sources of pollution, so it rendered certain animals unclean. No one quite knows what ancient wisdom or prejudice lay behind these dietary laws. Whether or not it was some primitive hygiene theory, it rendered certain animals, actions, persons and substances objectively unclean. Some of these taboos were carried over into Christianity with momentous consequences that still reverberate. For instance, it was taken for granted in the early Church that a menstrual woman should not take the sacrament. Peter Brown, in his book *The Body and Society*, pinpoints the issue admirably:

> Taboos taken from the book of Leviticus had been maintained by most Christians of the eastern Mediterranean. A third-century Bishop of Alexandria, a pupil of Origen, had written that it was unnecessary to tell menstruating women to keep away from the Eucharist: good Christian women did not need to be reminded of so obvious a prohibition. Temporary denial of access to the altar, due to menstruation and childbirth among women and to ejaculation among men, had underscored the position of human beings as creatures perched between nature and the city. They had protected human sacred space from the formless, purely biological, products of the body that periodically reminded the faithful of their indissoluble connection with the natural world.[2]

Long after this particular pollution taboo has been removed its influence is still felt. There are many Christians who are uncomfortable with women in sanctuary or choir, and find themselves incapable of receiving the sacrament from female administrators of the eucharistic bread and wine. For people of this particular tenderness, the thought of ordaining women to the priesthood is shudderingly unthinkable.

Seminal fluid was thought of as equally polluting, though there is one major difference we shall reflect upon presently. The ritual problems presented by seminal fluid are captured vividly in the first book of Samuel:

> Then came David to Nob to Ahimelech the priest: and Ahimelech came to meet David trembling, and said to him, 'Why are you alone, and no one with you?'
>
> And David said to Ahimelech the priest, 'The king has charged me with a matter, and said to me, "Let no one know anything of the matter about which I send you, and with which I have charged you." I have made an appointment with the young men for such and such a place. Now then, what have you at hand? Give me five loaves of bread, or whatever is here.'
>
> And the priest answered David, 'I have no common bread at hand, but there is holy bread; if only the young men have kept themselves from women.'
>
> And David answered the priest, 'Of a truth women have been kept from us as always when I go on an expedition; the vessels of the young men are holy, even when it is a common journey; how much more today will their vessels be holy?'
>
> So the priest gave him the holy bread; for there was no bread there but the bread of the Presence, which is removed from before the Lord, to be replaced by hot bread on the day it is taken away.
>
> (1 Sam. 21.1-6)

In subsequent Christian history this passage has been used to justify clerical celibacy with an almost geometrical neatness. It was put to me personally like this by a young monk over forty years ago: 'A catholic priest must celebrate mass every day. How could he do that purely if he'd had intercourse with his wife the night before? It follows, therefore, that priests who offer the eucharistic sacrifice daily must be celibate.'

Celibacy, of course, is achievable. However, we know from the literature of the desert fathers, and later volumes of moral theology, how difficult it was to deal with nocturnal emissions for those who followed the pollution theory. The general conclusion seemed to be that, while a nocturnal emission was physically polluting for a celibate and ought, therefore, to keep him from the Eucharist, it was not morally polluting and did not require confession unless he woke up and enjoyed it. Great dramas of the flesh and the spirit were fought in early Christianity over these issues, all of them vividly documented by Peter Brown in his magisterial study *The Body and Society*.

Nocturnal emissions aside, celibacy was achievable, at whatever cost, by the male. In theory a perfect state of ritual purity could be attained. But no woman by an act of will can renounce menstruation. We know, however, that certain ascetical practices carried to extremes inhibit ovulation. Studies of female marathon runners indicate that many of them stop menstruating. The same is true of anorexic women. This is probably what lies behind the ancient ascetical tradition that women consecrated to God, who eschewed their sexuality and disciplined their bodies severely, may occasionally be granted honorary male status.

Distant as these theories and practices are from our time, they still have a profound effect upon our conscious and unconscious attitudes, as well as upon the whole vocabulary of sexuality, liberally rehearsed in the tabloid press with its screaming headlines of 'Filthy pervert', 'Dirty beast'; not to mention the admonitory vocabulary of the Victorian boys' school with its obsession with smut and impurity, and its compulsive loathing of masturbation. It is particularly intriguing that we have carried this pollution theory of sexuality over from ancient times, because our Lord seems to have challenged and overturned it by his words and actions. He ignored most of the pollution taboos. He touched lepers and corpses; he allowed himself to be touched by women who were themselves in a high state of ritual impurity; and he inveighed against the hypocrisies of the whole ceremonial system. Presumably, this was not because he had anything in particular against washings and ritual cleansings, or lacked physical fastidiousness, but because he had penetrated to the heart of the matter, which was access to God and the Holy. Access to God was not something that was controlled by physical states of purity or impurity, by the avoidance of certain foods, articles of clothing, furniture, corpses or sanitary towels, but by purity of heart. He internalized value and virtue. He replaced an objective, ritualistic ethic of purity and pollution with an ethic of the heart and mind that demystified access to God.

It was a difficult lesson to learn and the early Church would probably have ignored it if it hadn't been for Paul. Something of the struggle that went on around this issue is reflected in Peter's vision at Joppa recounted in the Acts of the Apostles:

The next day, Peter went up on the housetop to pray, about the sixth hour. And he became hungry and desired something to eat; but while they were preparing it, he fell into a trance and saw the heaven opened, and something descending, like a great sheet, let down by four corners upon the earth. In it were all kinds of animals and reptiles and birds of the air. And there came a voice to him, 'Rise, Peter; kill and eat.' But Peter said, 'No, Lord; for I have never eaten anything that is common or unclean.' And the voice came to him again a second time, 'What God has cleansed, you must not call common.' This happened three times, and the thing was taken up at once to heaven.

(Acts 10.9-16)

It was this vision that prepared Peter for the entry of the Gentiles into the Christian community. The issue was essentially one of magic. The premise of magic is that access to God is achieved by manipulating the physical universe in such a way that one achieves power over the divine. It is a very deeply entrenched opinion in the human heart, and it is still fixed in the Christian tradition, in spite of the radical example of Jesus Christ. There are dualistic elements in Christianity, but no follower of Christ can be a dualist of the sort that sees the physical as the domain of the fallen one, and the body as the seat and laboratory of evil. It is the heart that is sick. It is our spirits that are confused and go wrong, not this poor Balaam's ass we call the body.

If we remove sexuality from this magical sphere, in which the sexual act is evaluated by a series of external criteria, similar in type to the dietary laws of the purity code, and replace it with an ethic of innerness and intention, how might we describe this new ethic and how might we promote it?

There is no doubt that the kind of superstitious sexual code we have been thinking about has had a profoundly restraining effect upon a volcanic instinct that is often destructive of human happiness. But the purity code itself has had a profoundly destructive effect upon human happiness. It was based upon a ritualized picture of reality that is no longer tenable. If there is a particularly Christian sexual ethic that we wish to commend today it will have to demonstrate its worth pragmatically, because we live in a society in which our bodily functions have been largely de-mystified. Let me now try to offer one possible interpretation of the Christian sexual ethic, before we explore some of the forces that make it so difficult to achieve.

The Christian traces everything back to God. God is both unity and relationship. There is relationship in God. This is what the doctrine of the Trinity means: there is, though the metaphor is clumsy, family life within the Godhead. The life of God is characterized by a self-giving exchange. The mutual surrender and love of the members of the Trinity preserve the unity of the divine nature.

It is our nature and destiny to be drawn to that same state. We are called to share in the divine nature. We seek that unity and relationship, that connectedness or wholeness, which is the life of God. Sexuality is a figure or symbol of our ultimate destiny with God, because it is a search for the other. We feel that it is not good for us to be alone. We feel mysteriously incomplete, so all our life is a searching for a remembered unity we have never yet known. Sexuality is one of the modes of our search; it is both a symptom of our incompleteness and a sign of our fulfilment. For the Christian, therefore, there are two ingredients in sexual experience. One is clearly a participation in the joy of God. We need not be afraid to rejoice in the pleasures of our bodily nature, but we must remember that these pleasures are the sign and seal of unity, relatedness, bondedness. For the Christian, sex should be part of a covenant between two persons, because it is a reflection or earthly representation of the covenant or marriage within the Godhead, and it is a reflection or earthly representation of the covenant or marriage between God and his people and Christ and his Church. Sex is the outward and visible sign of the mutual commitment that is achieved in a true relationship. Theoretically, human beings could achieve that level of commitment with more than one person. In fact, given our distracted and selfish nature, it does not work out like that. Made as we are, to succeed in developing trusting human relationships we need to concentrate; which is another way of saying we need to be faithful.

Christians try to live under the authority of a particular vision or revelation, though they often differ about how to. We are not compelled to do this. The vision is there, and we are drawn to it and try to grow into it. We believe that it is a vision of what is ultimately real. To conform to it, however slowly and painfully, is healthgiving and satisfying, because it conforms us to reality. To run against the grain of reality makes us unhappy, because it distorts us, gets us out of tune with things. The Christian vision of sexuality is extremely high and affirmative. When we reach the ideal at its highest representation, in truly surrendered and covenanted love, we are mirroring the very life of God. When we decline from that standard, we are going against the real grain of things and, in the long run, it tells on us.

Let me now try to draw some of these threads together. The source and origin of all things is a God in whom we are shown a pattern of covenanted love, in which there is an eternal rhythm of surrender and response, because it is love's nature to give. This dynamic and unceasing love expresses itself in the creation. God desires to make covenant with creation, with all created things, so that they might share the divine life. The Bible talks about this covenant as a marriage. God is married to Israel. But a pattern begins to assert itself: fidelity on the part of God, faithlessness on the part of Israel. This pattern of flight from covenant is called adultery in Scripture. We find it described with particular sternness in Jeremiah. Israel's sin is the worship of other Gods. To the God of Israel it is adultery, harlotry:

> You have played the harlot with many lovers; and would you return to me? says the Lord. Lift up your eyes to the bare heights and see! By the wayside you have sat awaiting lovers like an Arab in the

36

wilderness. You have polluted the land with your vile harlotry.

(Jer. 3.1-2)

In the same way, the children of God are called into covenanted relationships, called to pledge and bind themselves. And here the same pattern emerges. There seems to be something in us that pulls us away from faithfulness to our covenants. The symbol is continued in the New Testament. Christ likened himself to a bride. Paul talks about the importance of marriage, because 'it is like unto the marriage between Christ and his Church'. Here, too, the pattern emerges. We resist the covenant. We find it difficult to be faithful to Christ.

So we find a paradox. The drive of our nature is in the direction of covenant, of finding unity in relationship. But there is another law at work within us that pulls us away from our real joy. God works upon us to deepen our faithfulness, our ability to commit ourselves, by assuring us of the absolute security of God's love. Though we play the harlot, God will wait for us. God wants us to learn how to abide responsibly by our promises. Our promises or covenants are important for two reasons. First of all, it is in the nature of true love to bind itself, to make an avowal or pledge. Strong, confident love does this: it pledges itself in an act of surrender and commitment, not because the law requires it, but because it is in the nature of love to pledge itself into a new unity. But the vow or bond has a secondary function. There is something in us that works against the covenant desire, so the pledge acts as a restraint upon our weakness. It gives us power when we are at our weakest. In any human endeavour of value and significance there comes a moment when we are tempted to desert. It is here that our promise carries us. Vows help us in the dark corners and difficult places. Let me try to pull these claims into a single statement.

Full, bonded, faithful love is the image of the Trinity, and it is the desire of God for us in our sexual relations. This is the Christian ideal of sex. It is not simply achieved by taking marriage vows and living in strictly legal faithfulness. It is a dynamic ideal which may take the whole of a married lifetime to achieve.

What, then, about the unmarried? The Bible offers us the ideal and the Church ratifies the ideal in its official proclamation. Nevertheless, we live in an actual world and not some ideal world, and the Church has to deal with the world as it is, in all its complexity, failure and mystery. I would like to suggest a figure that might help us to measure the ideal content in diverse relationships.

Let us think, then, of sexuality as a continuum that stretches from the full, bonded solemnity of the theoretical ideal right across to the most casual sexual encounter. It is easy to judge the extreme cases. It is easy to see what is furthest from the ideal. This is casual promiscuity. Maybe it should be the object of our compassion, since much of it is a flight from loneliness: 'any comfort serves in a whirlwind', in Hopkins's phrase. Nevertheless, the Church cannot affirm it, even though it recognizes that there is hidden within it a spark of the divine longing. Let's come further along the continuum. There are relationships that are far from the ideal, but they have something of the ideal in them. Many love affairs are of this sort. There is a genuine, if disordered, love in them. A good example of this is found in one of Rose Macaulay's novels where one of the characters ruminates in these words:

> And then I thought how odd it was, all that love and joy and peace that flooded over me when I thought about him and how it all came from what was a deep meanness in our loves, for that is what adultery is, a meanness and a stealing, a taking away from someone what should be theirs, a great selfishness, and surrounded and guarded by lies lest it should be found out. And out of this meanness and this selfishness and this lying flow love and joy and peace, beyond anything that can be imagined. And this makes a discord in the mind, the happiness and the guilt and the remorse pulling in opposite ways so that the mind and soul are torn in two.[3]

Further up the continuum are those stable relationships between the unmarried, which have become a feature of our society, though they are not an exclusively modern phenomenon. Peter Brown tells us that they have a long history. Speaking of Augustine he writes:

> Unlike Alypius, Augustine plainly enjoyed sleeping with a woman. He opted for the next best thing to marriage — a strictly monogamous relationship with

a concubine. Such a relation was common in intellectual circles. It was accepted as valid even by Christians. An 'acceptable and often openly acknowledged sexual relationship, not covered by the law but with some rules of its own', concubinage was the very opposite of a dissolute arrangement. It lacked the essential ingredient of a legally valid marriage — the declared intention to produce legitimate offspring. It was frankly sexual. Augustine chose his companion because he loved her; and he slept with her because he loved to do so, and not so as to produce grandchildren for his mother or citizens for his home town. Since they had only one child in thirteen years, it seems more than likely that Augustine and his concubine practised birth-control of some kind.[4]

Many of these live-in relationships, ancient and modern, reflect many aspects of the ideal. There is a level of commitment and fidelity in them that is frequently publicly ratified in a marriage ceremony when children are desired. We can affirm much in these relationships, though we may not want to put the Church's seal of solemn approval upon them.

Finally, what about stable and pledged homosexual relationships? I think there are several grounds for offering a measure of affirmation. On our continuum they express several elements of the Christian ideal. First of all, they reflect something of the unitary and relational purpose of sexuality. In this area, as in others, we have to develop pastoral versatility and refuse to let the best be the enemy of the good. By this standard,

I have known committed homosexual relationships that have had redemptive value, because they have rescued people from the sadness and danger of casual and meaningless promiscuity. I find it difficult to believe that God does not rejoice in such evidence of growth. God is nursing us all up to perfect self-giving maturity and we all start from different places.

The place of the Christian homosexual in today's Church is one of peculiar difficulty and debate, and I would like at this point to digress onto the subject in some detail, before returning to the main theme. Before offering some opinions and interpretations, what facts or alleged facts are available to us?

First of all, it seems to be established in our society that a given percentage of the population, male and female, is constitutionally homosexual. We also know from a wide variety of personal testimonies that most homosexuals, because of their status as an unacceptable minority, go through a period of confusion, guilt, loneliness and self-hatred. The homosexual condition brings with it an intrinsic sense of being different from the rest of society, of being a moral outcast, often an object of fun, ridicule and hatred. In purely naturalistic terms we could probably account for this by pointing to the way most species attack outsiders or odd or weak members of their own group. However we account for it, 'gay-bashing', both physical and verbal, is a consistent theme in our culture. Most people, before they examine the issue, perceive the condition as abnormal, unnatural and therefore repulsive, or at least alien and puzzling. But to homosexuals it is their norm, their given nature; hence the bafflement and

41

anger they feel at finding themselves in such a cruel predicament.

Related to the homosexual experience of rejection is the sense of discomfort or revulsion felt by the uninformed member of the population at the existence of homosexuality. Even the most liberal-minded and accepting person would probably fail the 'what if?' test. Given that you would not reject your child if you discovered him or her to be gay, what if you were given a choice in the matter and could choose their sexual orientation? Most people would choose the 'norm', if only because it would rescue their child from inevitable pain. This, of course, is not a scientific judgement, but as a rough calculation it has merit, because it shows that there is a residual reserve about homosexuality that is almost automatic in even the most informed, educated, compassionate and liberal person. We can say, therefore, that to be gay is to be on the outside of society, and this must add a profound element of loneliness to gayness itself.

It is not surprising that the first response to a subjective awareness of being homosexual is usually a combination of fear and denial. It is, in Lord Alfred Douglas' famously tragic phrase, 'the love that dares not speak its name' or dares not in certain circles. The sexual instinct is a powerful energy, notoriously difficult to direct and govern, even where society accords it allowable expression. The originating impulse may have been the primordial urge to reproduce the species, and this may account for some of the alleged differences between male and female sexuality, but sexuality, like every other human instinct, has long since transcended its origin. The glory of humanity lies in the way it has elaborated each of the originating instincts into art and spiritual passion. Sexuality, though it continues to be the means by which the human race reproduces itself, has long since transcended its natural origin. It is something we enjoy for its own sake, but it is also a means to other good ends. The sharing of bodies can be the means whereby we begin to learn to share the deeper parts of ourselves. We know that children who are deprived of touch by their parents can grow up to be, quite literally, untouchable, people who flinch from real human contact; or they can become people who associate their sexuality, not with straightforward human warmth, but with some secret early experience of the touching they were starved of by their parents, like the man who could only achieve sexual arousal by wearing a plaster-cast during intercourse. The origin of this awkward sexual fetish lay in an emotionally starved childhood: 'At the age of eleven he broke his leg and while it was being set in the operating theatre it was held by an attractive young nurse. Excited by her hands touching his thigh, he had an erection on the operating table.'[5] Thereafter he associated his sexual longings with that moment of contact and became fixated on it.

The dilemma our sexuality places us in lies between the dangers of denial or dependence. We can be so afraid of our sexuality that we shut it away like a mad relative in the cellar, where it secretly dominates our life. Human integration begins when we acknowledge its presence, no matter how unacceptable it may be to us. This is a part of the complex Christian experience we call repentance. We own who we are, including our hitherto nameless fears and longings. Many homosexuals, especially if they were brought up in a Christian tradition that taught them to understand homosexual longings as sinful, spend years in a painful denial of their real nature; only when they are encouraged to acknowledge and bless it as part of themselves do they discover the real peace of self-acceptance. To sit with a group of Christians who happen to be gay and hear their stories of pain and self-hatred, as they give an account of their life in the Church, is a chastening as well as a moving experience. Many gay Christians have used the language of grace to describe their journey from denial and fear into self-acceptance and the courage to reach out in love to others, yet the Church has usually taught them that it is only comfortable with them when they are inhabiting the state of secret but silent pain. This is because the Church is more afraid of the dangers of excess, of dependence upon sex, than of the dangers of denial. It would rather deal with the quiet sorrows of death than the noisy problems of life. But in our day many gay Christians are challenging this conspiracy of silence. They insist that we look at them and listen to their experience as men and women, committed to the Christian pilgrimage, who happen to be gay.

Some of them, like their counterparts in the heterosexual majority, will decide that the most creative way to handle the reality of their own nature is by the difficult discipline of celibacy. Others, however, will prefer to make the same choice as most heterosexuals and express their sexual needs in affectionate relationships. Like everyone else, they will be tempted, on occasion, to misuse or misapply their sexuality, but they will recognize the temptation as a consequence of their imperfect humanity and will refuse to accord it more or less importance than it deserves. Above all, they will recognize that human behaviour is not validated or invalidated by a fixed 'natural' principle but by a humanizing principle that transcends mere nature. This evolutionary approach may appear to contradict Scripture and will, of course, be forced to repudiate those aspects of Scripture that reflect, not knowable divine truth, but the social and cultural context of the time in which the truth was expressed. But there is no escape from this dilemma anyway. We either treat Scripture ahistorically, denying everything we know about its origin and development, or we treat it heuristically, recognizing that God's mystery comes through it, but has to be searched for and interpreted and can no longer be read off like an automatic computer print-out. This approach will certainly plunge us into areas of uncertainty and the perils of freedom, but it is more consonant with the gospel of grace and forgiveness than the automatic theories of divine direction that the fundamentalists offer in its place.

Scriptural references on the subject of homosexuality are, in fact, very sparse, the two main texts being in Leviticus 20 which tells us, 'If a man lies with a man as with a woman both of them have committed an abomination. They shall be put to death. Their blood is upon us' (Lev. 20.13). And, in the New Testament, in Romans 1.26-7: 'For this reason God gave them up to dishonourable passions. Their women exchanged natural relations for unnatural, and the men likewise gave up natural relations with women and were consumed with passion for one another, men committing shameless acts with men and receiving in their own persons the due penalty for their error.' As I have already suggested, much will depend upon our theory of biblical interpretation as we approach these texts, but there is scarcely any doubt that the Bible as it stands seems sternly to disapprove of same sex activities. So the immediate and most common perception of the biblical attitude is profoundly unsympathetic towards the homosexual condition. Alongside this undeniable fact we must place the emergence, in this century, of an understanding of homosexuality, not as a chosen perversion to add spice to a jaded sexual norm, but as a permanent orientation, a fixed normative variation, to which scriptural references are irrelevant, if it is held that they refer to homosexual activity by heterosexuals for thrills or for some other reason. If a moral act is at least partly defined by the intention of the agent then, it is alleged, there must be a difference between a homosexual relationship between gay people who love each other and a homosexual act perpetrated by a heterosexual out of violence, lust or thrill-seeking.

Christians, including Christian theologians, are in notorious disagreement in all these matters, but that is precisely the point. There does not seem to be, at the moment, a consensus of opinion among Christians on this subject. There seem to be four current attitudes held in the Christian community so, as a matter of fact, we have to acknowledge that there is a range of Christian opinion on the subject. According to the Westminster *Dictionary of Christian Ethics* there are four broad attitudes to homosexuality among Christians. First of all, there are the punitive rejectors who would treat it as both a crime and a sin and punish it, though it is doubtful if many of them would actually insist upon the implementation of the Levitical purity code in sentencing to death homosexuals caught *in flagrante delicto*. Next there are non-punitive objectors who would always treat homosexual relations as sinful, but not as criminal. An apt parallel would be adultery, which is no longer a statutory offence in this country, though the Christian Church and most public opinion holds it to be a sin. The third group are qualified accepters who would probably seek to apply the norm of monogamous sexuality to gay people, as well as to heterosexuals. And they would claim that by this acceptance or permission, many gay people have established stable relationships that have rescued them from loneliness and the promiscuity that has often characterized their search for love and companionship. Finally, there is a group, probably a small group, of total accepters, who believe that gay people should create their own norm and not be dictated to by a section of the population that can have no real inner knowledge of their condition.

If we were dealing only with lay Christians the problem would resolve itself in a pragmatic way. Unordained gay Christians would continue, as they do now, to locate themselves in Christian communities where they find a measure of acceptance and trust. They would, for that reason, avoid most evangelical churches, because there they would be held to be living in a kind of structural sinfulness that was inconsistent with Christian discipleship. It is this fact that creates the profoundest irony in the current situation, because it is the evangelical wing of the Church that knows least about homosexuality and yet shouts loudest about it, a kind of disproportion that is not unknown in other spheres of human prejudice and bigotry. It is probably true that most lay Christians who happen to be homosexual find a reasonable level of acceptance in the Christian community, even though they may have to search for congenial congregations. The real heart of the problem for the Church emerges because of the incidence of homosexuality among clergy. It is difficult to quantify this, but it seems to be higher than the norm in the population at large, and there may be several reasons for this. Christianity, at least in its Scriptures and in its best aspirations, is a religion for outcasts and sinners, so it is hardly surprising that a despised and rejected section of society finds an extraordinary echo of its condition in the life of one who was himself despised and rejected, and who yet consorted with outcasts and sinners. Secondly, and at the risk of stereotyping the homosexual, it has been observed that the homosexual character, if such a thing can be said to exist in its perfect state, is often sensitive to spiritual realities, to beauty, to innerness. This must be a contributory factor to the large number of homosexual poets, musicians and actors who have glorified the Western cultural tradition. Indeed, a sort of sub-group of this larger aesthetic impulse can be found in the Anglo-Catholic tradition, where many homosexuals have found a highly congenial expression of their faith. Statistics, as usual, are hard to confirm or validate, but that there is a solid connection between the Anglo-Catholic tradition and homosexuality is fairly well established.

The reasons for this connection may be complex, but it clearly has something to do with the aesthetic sensitivity we have already alluded to. Many of the great leaders and saints of the Anglo-Catholic movement have been constitutionally homosexual, though celibate in their practice, and they have been men of great pastoral and spiritual gifts, often prepared to take jobs that their married counterparts would not even entertain. This is still true today. Homosexual priests are often to be found doing valiant work in UPAs and inner-city neighbourhoods. Because they are vulnerable men, touched with infirmity and to some extent strangers and exiles upon earth, they often make good and sensitive counsellors for the spiritually frail, the guilt-ridden, the depressed and the rejected. Without them the Church would have been far poorer than it has been. We can probably be fairly certain that, until comparatively recently, most homosexual clergy would have been celibate in aspiration, intention and usually in practice. The sexually active gay priest is a new phenomenon. The current climate of opinion makes it difficult to establish facts in this area, but we are not talking about a minority who may be sexually chaotic in their practices, but about a group who have committed, settled relationships that intentionally approach the Christian norm of marriage. Such men and women would argue for a Christian understanding of sexuality as sacramental, as the sign and reinforcement of deep personal commitment. They would claim a place for themselves on the continuum of sexual relationships I have tried to describe.

If we accept this figure of the continuum, it allows us to celebrate the authoritative ideal in its fullness, without departing from it as the Church's standard, while allowing us to affirm much that is good and redemptive in relationships that may not yet fully reflect the ideal itself. We must in this, as in all things, affirm as much as we can in people, as they struggle towards maturity. But there are many factors that work against the achievement of the ideal and a wise pastoral theology will take them into account. Let us look at some of them.

On the biological level sex is a raw power or instinct. It is at its most potent when we are least able to cope emotionally and psychologically with it. In a young adolescent male hormones are zooming round like jet fighters, which the young man, unless he is powerfully motivated, is almost incapable of handling well. The head of a famous family planning institute, who is by no means traditional in her attitude to sexuality, has gone on record as saying, with a humour that's more than tinged with reality, that she wished she could figure out a way to keep adolescent boys from getting at adolescent girls. In less complicated societies than ours the matter sorted itself out in a naturalistic way.

In our society, where puberty seems to come earlier and earlier, and marriage is postponed later and later, it is very difficult for the young to handle their sexuality wisely, as the statistics and consequences of teenage sex demonstrate. All that I am trying to note here is the powerful nature of the sexual urge and how difficult it is to modify or restrain it, unless society structures itself in an inhibiting way. Claims are frequently made that previous epochs in human history were more chaste, but one can probably dispose of the claims by pointing to the lack of sexual opportunity in those societies. It has been observed that the invention of the motor car and access to it by North American teenagers did more to transform sexual practices in the United States than any other single factor, except the emergence of birth control techniques. If the opportunity presents itself, human beings will act out their sexuality, unless they are inhibited by interior factors and private restraints.

In the past a number of external factors had a restraining effect on sexuality, but they have lost much of their force today. These external restraints were once described as *detection*, *infection* and *conception*. The danger of being found out, the danger of catching a sexually transmitted disease and the danger of conceiving a child, all imposed external restraints upon men and women, and to some extent still do. The AIDS epidemic has added a new urgency to this purely practical argument for restraint, but these consequential elements do not actually help the moral argument along, though they may have a profound effect upon actual human behaviour. We must ask, 'What would an appropriate sexual ethic be for me in a society in which neither infection nor conception were dangers?' In other words, we must search for a human ethic that is intentional, rooted in the heart and not one that is merely contingent or consequential. One only has to say that, of course, in order to see its naivety and how unlikely it is of achievement. Nevertheless, the ethic itself ought to be able to stand on its own. We must also remember that it will always be an ethic of aspiration, as in any other department of human moral activity. Our aspirations draw us forward. They provide us with a guiding light in the distance to struggle towards. Other types of moral aspiration are used in this way, but, as we have already seen, the area of sexuality is peculiarly loaded, and sexual failure seems to attract a disproportionate obloquy.

Another important fact in understanding sexuality is the recognition that the sexual instinct seems to be peculiarly vulnerable to misdirection. Sometimes this takes a victimless form. In some people orgasm is intrinsically associated with apparently unrelated external factors, such as punishment rituals, clothes fetishes or bodily elimination routines. We know, for instance, that otherwise mature and normal men will pay women to dress up in gym slips or black leather outfits and cane them, or act out other school-room charades of discipline. The range of sexual pathologies should call forth from us more compassion than condemnation, particularly for those sad creatures who can only achieve sexual satisfaction by the purchase of elaborately staged scenarios of humiliation and abuse that must speak of some tragic inner wounding. The list of sexual variables seems endless.

This fact already points to the emotional and psychological loading that sexuality bears, but there is another aspect of it we ought to note. In spite of the claims made by sexual utopians in the 1960s, sex is never value-free, never without its human and emotional consequences. Sex may be fun, but it is unpredictable and mysterious fun. Mary Calderone put it well when she said, 'The girl plays at sex, for which she is not ready, because fundamentally what she wants is love; and the boy plays at love, for which he is not ready, because what he wants is sex.' Sex is not just about sex. This is why all societies and religious systems have sought some kind of control and ordering of the thing. We may turn a blind eye to victimless sexual activities of which we disapprove, but we cannot ignore sexual practices that are based on oppression and exploitation of the weak and unconsenting, such as rape, child abuse and even bestiality. Because the light that enlightens us all casts its own shadow, sexuality has its dark side.

Another element whose impact is difficult to evaluate or measure is the shame factor that seems to be a product of Judaeo-Christianity, though is not exclusive to it. There is a powerful shame associated with sexual frailty in our culture, reflected in the tabloid obsession with the sexual activities of public figures. In ancient Christian thought this shame had its origin in Adam's transgression. Before the fall Adam and Eve existed in a state in which sexuality, as we understand it, did not exist. It was not until they had fallen that they knew they were naked. St Augustine wrestled with this theme more intricately than any other thinker of his time. He was persuaded that Adam and Eve, had they never fallen, would have propagated children without what he called concupiscence, the fateful desire that accompanied sexuality.

> An urge which burns quite indiscriminately for objects allowed and disallowed; and which is bridled by the urge for marriage, that must depend upon it, but that restrains it from what is not allowed . . . Against this drive, which is in tension with the *law of the mind*, all chastity must fight: that of the married couple, so that the urge of the flesh may be rightly used, and that of continent men and virgins, so that, even better and with a struggle of greater glory, it should not be used at all. This urge, had it existed in Paradise . . . would, in a wondrous pitch of peace, have never run beyond the bidding of the will . . . It would never have forced itself upon the mind with thoughts of inappropriate and impermissible delights. It would not have had to be held upon the leash by married moderation, or fought to a draw by ascetic labor. Rather, when once called for, it would have followed the will of the person with all the ease of a single-hearted act of obedience.[6]

In other words, sexual intercourse would have had all the passion of an act of artificial donor insemination. But even this would have been too much for some of the Fathers. According to Peter Brown, Augustine would have appeared dangerously revisionist to other

Christian Fathers such as Ambrose, Jerome and Gregory of Nyssa. Augustine, with a sort of tormented pragmatism, tried to find a place for the immutable fact of human sexuality in marriage. His own sexuality caused him deep inner conflict, but he recognized that without it human society could not endure. Absolutist celibates like Jerome, Gregory of Nyssa and Ambrose were alive and therefore able to promote their theories, because they themselves were the fruit of sexual desire. Even so, they were in no doubt about its fallen status. Peter Brown writes:

> All three had shared an instinctive, largely un-analysed, assumption about the origins of marriage and of sexuality. Marriage, intercourse and Paradise were as incompatible, in their minds, as were Paradise and death. Of that, at least, they felt they could be certain.
>
> This meant that sexuality, hence marriage and the creation of the family, could only have followed the Fall of Adam and Eve. They were the result of a sad decline, by which Adam and Eve had lapsed from an 'angelic' state into physicality, and so into death. A question mark was allowed to hover over human society. Marriage, and the structures that sprang from it, could not be derived from the original nature of the human person. Ascetic exegesis of the Fall of Adam and Eve tended to preserve, at the back of the minds of its exponents, a lingering doubt: society, marriage, and, if not those, certainly sexual inter-course, were fundamentally alien to the original definition of humanity. They had come as an

55

afterthought. They had imposed limitations on the first angelic majesty of Adam and Eve.[7]

St Gregory the Great followed Augustine in his pragmatism. He dismissed the Levitical taboos and focused his attention on the will. Peter Brown goes on:

A follower of Augustine in his magnificent obsession with the will, Gregory turned his back on that tradition. Neither the woman's blood nor the man's semen counted for anything. The 'primitive nation of the English' must be told that what kept human beings away from the sacred had nothing to do with their physical bodies. It was the subtle, impalpable flaw within the human will that stood between them and God. The dislocation of the will caused telltale eddies of 'illicit delight' to form in the wake of every act of married intercourse. Such delight was no longer seen as an eminently physical experience, caused by the exuberant rush of vital spirit through the veins; it lingered, rather, as a sharp, sweet flicker in the heart. Pious Romans, Gregory added, usually kept away from church until such feelings had subsided in their minds. They did not do so because their bodies had emitted seed. Will and memory, topics of absorbing interest to thinkers of an introspective turn of mind, and not the body, were at stake: 'For, behold, this is what it is to be human . . . a creature with a will, at once bound and free.'[8]

However we account for the phenomenon, whether it is caused in men physiologically, by their sense of depletion and spentness after coition, or in women, at least on occasions, by the sense of being used as mere receptacles, or by some sense of shame that the will is still subject to the tyranny of physical delight, post-coital sadness is a fact liberally attested in literature. Sometimes it is a blazing sense of shame, sometimes merely a sense of loss:

Th' expense of spirit in a waste of shame
Is lust in action; and, till action, lust
Is perjured, murd'rous, bloody, full of blame,
Savage, extreme, rude, cruel, not to trust;
Enjoyed no sooner but despised straight;
Past reason hunted, and no sooner had,
Past reason hated as a swallowed bait
On purpose laid to make the taker mad;
Mad in pursuit, and in possession so;
Had, having, and in quest to have, extreme;
A bliss in proof, and proved, a very woe.
Before, a joy proposed; behind, a dream.
   All this the world well knows, yet none knows well
   To shun the heaven that leads men to this hell.[9]

However we expound it, the Christian loading of sexual activity with theological significance has made it more momentous than other human instincts and their confusions. And here I would like to slip in a personal reflection. Like many boys of my generation and social class, I was brought up in a rather macho society. Even before I became a Christian, I had been unconsciously formed into an attitude to women that saw them as traps, as sources of physical and moral enfeeblement. My favourite uncle was a Royal Marine, who married later than most men, and he often used to joke about how women tied you down. In my boyish romanticism I saw marriage as a kind of surrender of the will, a binding of the strong and lonely male. My favourite films were all about strong and silent drifters, who rode into lonely towns in the North American West and cleaned out the baddies. Towards the end of the film the local beauty would plead with the hero to stay and settle down with her, and he would be sorely tempted; but come sun-up he would be seen saddling his black stallion behind the ranch. He would mount his horse and ride off alone, because a man had to do what a man had to do. There was something shaming and weak in the men who stood beside their wives behind the picket fences and waved at the lonely hero, as he became small against the vast western sky. When I became a Christian, I transposed this theme into a Christian key and called it celibacy. My heroes became monks, men who had spurned the softening pleasures of the world for the high, lonely plains of the spirit. Yet, accompanying both of these phases of my development there was always a fascination with and a profound attraction towards women, and a crushing, if unadmitted, sexual urge. I remember telling a friend, another trainee monk, that if I ever married I felt I would cease to be able to pray. Looking back, I can see that when I did marry I tried to live and work like a married celibate. I paid more attention to my professional than to my family responsibilities, because I felt that was what I was for essentially. My domestic responsibilities must never be allowed to crowd out the professional ones. Indeed, it became a point of defensive pride in me to demonstrate that in no way would marriage inhibit my total commitment to my vocation.

It is obvious that sexuality for Christians is a profoundly fated area. Our sexuality is intricate and convoluted, and creative of pain and torment as well as of ecstasy. Yet, sexuality can also be straightforwardly enjoyable. It is not entirely naive to believe in the possibility of an affectionate, unmomentous sexuality that is theoretically non-exploitative. Nevertheless, there is a human tendency towards bonding and exclusivity, of which coition is what sacramental theologians would call an effective sign, an activity that effects what it also signifies, union. Even if we remove the metaphysical profundity from sexuality, it is worth noting that we can come close to the traditional understanding of chastity from a purely pragmatic perspective. In Latin chastity is *integritas*. It suggests integrity or single-mindedness. There is a high distraction and destruction quotient in sexuality: it can do violence to relationships, it can ruin careers, it can take one's mind off things on which one's mind ought to be. So there is always something of a struggle towards integrity, a unity of being between will and heart. It is possible to do the right thing for the right reason; to restrain oneself, not out of superstition or the wrong kind of God-hauntedness, but because it makes human sense, because there are other things to be done, because life is bigger than sex.

Finally, we must recognize that there are certain professions or states of life that are particularly premised upon human trust, such as the ordained ministry, the medical and teaching professions. People in these positions are strategically placed to exploit others for their own sexual gratification, so there has to be a code for the protection of the weak. In every profession there is a danger of insider-trading, and those professions that are particularly exposed to the vulnerability, loneliness and despair of others must be especially sensitive to the danger of exploitation.

This is an extremely difficult area for clergy to deal with. Being close to the vulnerable as we often are, it is doubly important for us to know our own wounds. There are two contrasting sets of dangers we are exposed to. The first is to operate with weak or non-existent sexual boundaries and exploit the relationships of trust and affection we develop with others. We can use them to solace our own needs. This can take the form of physical seduction, but emotional seduction can be just as, if not more, dangerous.

The opposing danger is to be so afraid of our own sexual vulnerability that we enclose ourselves in emotional armour plating, so that no one can touch us. Any effective pastoral relationship calls for tenderness, and to be tender and warm necessitates coming to terms with our own emotional and sexual nature. There are no more tragic figures in life and in literature than the cold and lonely figures who are so afraid of the fires in their own hearts that they would put them out rather than run the danger of being burned by them.

Notes

1 W. B. Yeats, 'Crazy Jane talks to the Bishop'.
2 Peter Brown, *The Body and Society* (Faber & Faber 1988), pp. 433ff.
3 Rose Macaulay, *The Towers of Trebizond* (Collins 1965), p. 253.
4 Brown, op. cit., p. 390.
5 From an article in *The Independent*, 21 January 1992.
6 Brown, p. 424.
7 Brown, p. 399.
8 Brown, p. 434.
9 William Shakespeare, Sonnet 129.

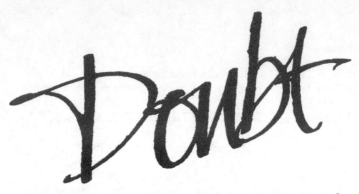

Doubt is the subjective state of uncertainty as to the truth or reality of anything, according to one of the Oxford dictionaries. It is a painful and possibly tragic state, but it also offers immensely comic opportunities to irreverent observers. Doubt has provided a rich theme for English novelists. One of the central characters in A. N. Wilson's Victorian pastiche *Gentlemen in England* offers a touching yet amusing picture of a sombre Victorian who had lost his faith, the rest of whose life was an act of mourning. Compton Mackenzie, in his series of novels about Anglo-Catholicism, explored a very rarefied sub-section of doubt in his accounts of Anglican clergy who come increasingly to doubt the validity of their own Orders and the Catholicity of the Church of England. This is a steady theme in Anglican experience. We still read of disenchanted Anglican priests who convert to Roman Catholicism because of their doubts about the Anglican Church. The comic possibilities of these states of mind are appreciated only if one is distanced from the difficulty. If one is a healthy-minded and contented atheist, the sight of an ex-minister gloomily dragging his way through life, because he had ceased to believe in the existence of God, can be very entertaining. Or if one's religious convictions are of a broad and generous type, laced with large elements of scepticism, a grown man agonizing about whether he has been validly ordained and can genuinely say the words that will create the real presence of Christ in the bread and the wine of the Eucharist, is a subject of some merriment. Some people are by nature too sceptical to appreciate the painfulness of the struggle between faith and doubt. It is also true that some believers make faith absurd by their supernatural scrupulousness and anxiety over unverifiable metaphysical claims.

Nevertheless, doubt is a potent source of stress for many believers, especially in the ordained ministry, where there is a tacit expectation that clergy inhabit a doubt-free zone. Doubt can be a difficulty for clergy in different ways. Super-confident believers among the clergy can be intimidating to searchers and doubters. However, it is almost certainly the case that some of the most confident over-believers are running from their own unacknowledged doubts. This is a slippery subject, of course, but there often seems to be an inverse relationship between vehement pronunciation and inner certainty. That was why Bertrand Russell remarked that zeal was a bad mark for a cause. No one was zealous about the two times table. People are zealous about things they are not quite or cannot be quite sure about. Their anxiety leads them to a compensatory exaggeration.

We recognize the phenomenon in other areas. We know, for instance, that some of the most passionate crusaders against vice are themselves deeply troubled about their own sexuality. Sometimes this contradiction is expressed in a straightforwardly hypocritical way, where public figures denounce actions they are secretly engaged in themselves. The most dramatic recent incidence of this phenomenon has been provided by the sexual careers of certain well-known tele-evangelists in the USA, who were violently identified with the puritanism of the 'moral majority'. Famous for their public denunciation of immorality, they were discovered to be adulterers or consorters with prostitutes in their private lives. This kind of blatant contradiction is rarer than the more complex phenomenon presented by the person who is running from the knowledge of his or her own nature. The pain of this unadmitted inner struggle is often transposed into ostentatious public denunciation of the very part of the person's inner nature he or she most fears. This is a theme well visited in literature and drama. One of the most vivid recent expressions of it was in *The Offence*, a film about a young man accused of violent sexual offences against girls. He is brutally interrogated by a police officer, played by Sean Connery, who ends up beating him to death because, as the film makes plain, he is himself immensely troubled by violent sexual fantasies about girls. In the person of the suspect he kills that part of his own nature which he fears and refuses to come to terms with. All of which should demonstrate to us the need to know our own doubts, especially the unadmitted ones; or at least to achieve empathy with the doubts of others, even if we do not share them.

Another danger that faces clergy comes, not from a reluctance to address doubt, but from a public fixation with it. Clergy can become obsessed with what they perceive to be the naive beliefs of their parishioners, which they seek to disturb at any cost. This usually takes the form of repeated assaults upon the uncritical acceptance of the historic truth of the gospels, usually focused on the accounts of the virgin birth or the empty tomb. It is, of course, possible to believe in these matters in the wrong way, or with unnecessary passion; but it is equally possible to become obsessed with their historical unreliability and to expect a precision in understanding and language about them that is unattainable.

These are mere quibbles, of course, compared to the great enterprise associated with the name of the Cambridge theologian Don Cupitt, who is engaged in a quixotic campaign to convert Christianity to atheism, no matter how complex and religious a version of atheism it may turn out to be. Don Cupitt seems to have gone from doubt about the reality of God to complete certainty about the unreality of God. He provides us with a good example of the way doubt can hijack and torment an ordained minister. Having become persuaded that the religious enterprise is an exclusively human construct, with no reference to an external divine reality, he has now embarked upon a passionate missionary exercise to convert the Church to his brand of atheism. The comic possibilities in this enterprise ought to be considerable. However, Mr Cupitt himself is far from being a comic figure. Indeed, it has to be said that he is a rather humourless one. Nevertheless, the sight of such a Savonarola of the intellect striving to convert corrupt and lazy Christians to his own arduous form of religious unbelief is highly entertaining. I fear, however, that when the movie is finally made it won't be a lot of fun. There is much wit but little humour in the script.

And that is not as irrelevant an aside as we might believe, because humour is an important element in faith. Humour is a sense of proportion, allied to an awareness of the incongruousness of many human claims and occasions. Humour can rescue us from our own obsessions, whether of overbelief or unbelief, just as it can rescue us from a self-important absorption in our own sinfulness.

> Once in a saintly passion
> I cried with desperate grief,
> 'O Lord, my heart is black with guile;
> Of sinners I am chief.'
>
> Then stooped my guardian angel
> And whispered from behind,
> 'Vanity, my little man!
> You're nothing of the kind.'[1]

Our commitment to the great enterprise of faith and understanding should be irradiated with the humour that recognizes the incongruousness as well as the courage of this small naked biped, *homo sapiens*, seeking to understand and explain the mysteries of the universe.

So far we have been thinking about *religious* doubt and it will obviously be the main focus of this chapter. Nevertheless, it is misleading when people automatically associate doubt with religion. There is an intrinsic connection between faith and doubt, but faith and doubt are human experiences, human realities, before they are theological or spiritual states, and we ought to go back to this human sense of the word before enquiring further into its theological status. The fact is that even in a provably Godless universe, faith and doubt would continue to exist, because they characterize every aspect of human life and not simply the spiritual aspect. If we look at human beings we will discover some who are constitutionally trusting and some who are constitutionally sceptical. We are confronted yet again with one of those continuums along which people find themselves. The continuum is defined at each pole by a paradigm of trust and a paradigm of doubt.

There are trusting types who believe us, take our word for things. They are people of an affirming and accepting disposition, who believe that we are innocent until proved guilty and our guilt would take a lot of proving. One way to describe such people is to say that they give us the benefit of the doubt, and that is a very significant use of language. The phrase refers to those situations that lack clarity and decidedness. If we are caught in a dispute about our own trustworthiness, and the cases for and against us are equally balanced, the trusting person will give us the benefit of the doubt, will place the casting vote on our side; whereas the sceptical person will vote the other way and the casting vote will go against us. It is the same evidence that is before the trusting person and the doubting person: but, as always in human situations, the personal perspective of the beholder influences the outcome, sometimes decisively. Trusting people have other characteristics than a sympathetic attitude towards people on trial. Their positive, accepting and upbeat approach influences their whole attitude to life. They are more likely to be experimental and innovative, prepared to try out new things. At their most enthusiastic and optimistic they can be a trial to their more reserved and sceptical colleagues, because they tend to present a new enthusiasm or guru to the attention of their friends every month. This can be depressing to those who have settled comfortably into one of life's bunkers, from which they view the insanity of the universe with melancholy satisfaction.

There are lots of ironies to note here. No human typology captures its subjects perfectly, but an intricacy that is worth observing is the paradox of theological conservatives, who claim to be maximalist in their beliefs (the phrase 'full faith' is often used of them) but who are actually operating from a sceptical base, though their scepticism is exclusively reserved for new ideas and practices. It is one of the more piquant ironies of current debate in the Church that the people who claim to be the real believers often seem to be operating from a rather weary and defensive perspective on life. They are like people who don't expect much good to come of anything any more. They have grown used to the old words and the old formulas from which they derive a kind of security, so they become passionately engaged in defending them against what they take to be the assaults of the neophiliacs, who believe that things new as well as old can be brought out of God's treasure chest and who enthusiastically leap on passing bandwagons because you never know what exciting place you might end up in.

If we accept some elements of this characterization, we can arrive at the paradoxical perspective that reveals the men and women who promote change in Church and society as the people of faith; whereas the conservatives who claim to be passionate believers in the full faith and the old values appear to be motivated more by doubt of the new than trust in the old. As we might expect from a knowledge of the psychological convolutions of the human soul, it is very often inner doubt and melancholy that leads to defensiveness in matters of faith. There is an important sense in which the courage to trust and risk comes from a profoundly rooted knowledge that we are loved and accepted. It is this original endowment of love that gives us the ability to take risks and to try out the new. Sometimes this fascination for the new is a kind of shallowness, bred of boredom, a hectic need to be up to something different; but often it is bred of a deep trust. The most captivating version of this profound trustingness has been revealed in very old, very holy people, such as Pope John XXIII, Michael Ramsey and Brother Roger at Taizé. In their old age they continued to be open to the new; they continued to relate warmly to the young and they continued to surprise the Church. John XXIII called Taizé 'God's little springtime'. It is the hopefulness of spring that characterizes the trusting person.

At the other end of the continuum we find the sceptics, the critical types who perform the useful function of subjecting every idea or institution to a withering and critical test. If they exist in an institution we wish to change, we have to convert them, isolate them or ignore them. They are the ones who will see the drawbacks in any scheme we propose. They will subject it to an unanswerable critical interrogation. In some cases their critical faculties are used as legitimate tools to test ideas and institutions. If the test is weathered and the claim proved, they will come aboard in some capacity. They may even become enthusiastic exponents of it, but they are rarely found in the front line of the cavalry charge of new ideas.

There is another type of sceptic whose scepticism is more than a technique for testing the spirits. It is a kind of psychic immobility that will not be persuaded, even though one were to rise from the dead. Most human endeavours of any significance call for action without assured certainty of outcome. The immobilist doubter is incapable of making this kind of leap. What immobilist doubters want is a risk-free universe, a universe in which the future is completely predictable. Since this is impossible, immobilist doubters stay put. They are the kind of people who won't let their children go into the water until they learn to swim. By their catchphrases you shall know them: 'It won't work here'; 'The last fellow tried that and it failed'; 'We are good at cutting people down to size in this parish'.

Trusters and doubters have their advantages and disadvantages. The disadvantage that trusters face is that they can be easily exploited by snake oil salesmen and other con artists. Since they always give the benefit of the doubt, they are suckers for a sales pitch. They will buy thermal underwear in a heatwave. At their most insidiously gullible they have a tendency towards dependency on the strong, maybe even a need to follow the leader. History is full of examples of strong, mad and magnetic leaders who led their suggestible followers to hell. Adolph Hitler exploited this tendency on a massive scale. Jim Jones, who led his followers to a commune in Guyana and prevailed upon them to commit mass suicide one afternoon, did the same thing on a smaller scale. There are people, movements and ideas that we can trust, but there are probably just as many that we ought to doubt. Natural trusters contribute their share to the creation of circumstances in which evil flourishes. Leaders of institutions can sometimes be hypnotized by charismatic charlatans whose deadly advice can damage or destroy the institutions they serve. Rasputin played his part in the overthrow of the Russian state and helped to change the pattern of world history, because of his power over the Tsar and Tsarina, whose anxiety for their haemophiliac son overrode their political prudence. Trust can be pathological, it can be invested in people and movements that do not deserve it.

But trusters have many advantages. They can make things happen, because they are not afraid of change. They can inject into a tired institution a new sense of possibility and hope. Their most precious gift is an almost psychic ability to discern the future. In business and commerce they predict trends and waves of fashion in food and clothing, in ideas and political styles, even in theological developments. They dream dreams and see visions, and very often bring their visions to pass. If you study the bookstalls in airport terminals you will find a whole sub-section of literature dedicated to this experience. These are the 'How to' and 'Can do' books. They tell how entrepreneurs, by sheer energy, enthusiasm and hopefulness, turned decaying industrial concerns into multi-national companies. They promise courses on how to turn diffident, unassertive, psychological wimps into world-beaters and go-getters. The books will be full of positive thinking and exercises in self-suggestion, full of case histories illustrating the importance of a right attitude and a positive spirit to success in any field. These books sell in their millions and they bear testimony to the importance of an affirming spirit. They are all about faith. It may be only ourselves they tell us to believe in, but they do most assuredly believe in belief. Many of them, of course, come from the USA, which, unlike Britain, is a believing culture; that is to say, it is a culture that believes in belief, believes in the importance of self-motivation, believes that things are meant to go on getting better. Anyone who has worked on the other side of the Atlantic will recognize the syndrome. It is one that patronizing and superior Brits frequently sneer at. The fact remains that for all its crassness and naivety, the American experiment is a colossal testimony to the importance of faith in human life.

Americans believe in things, such as the flag and the American way of life, the right to get rich, the possibility of finding happiness. They also believe, we might even say they overbelieve, in religion, but it's probably more accurate to say they believe in *belief*. One of the most useful books on North American religious sociology in the 1950s, *Protestant, Catholic and Jew*, written by Will Herberg, was a study of American religiosity. It concluded that Americans believed in belief in God more than they believed in God. In other words, it didn't much matter what you believed in as long as you believed in something, because human beings could not live without something to believe in. And there's much to be said for that point of view.

There is a perceptive and entertaining book on sale in the USA at the moment called *Brit Think, Ameri Think*.[2] It compares and contrasts American and British culture. One of the conclusions the book arrives at, which neatly illustrates the difference in attitude between the two allies, is that Americans don't believe in death, they fight against it, resist it, try to remain eternally young, something for which they are often sneered at by the British. But the book goes on to point out that while it is probably true that Americans don't believe in death, it is equally true that the British don't believe in life. The Venerable John Henry Newman got it right when he wrote in *The Grammar of Assent*: 'Life is for action. If we insist on proofs for everything we shall never come to action: to act you must assume and that assumption is faith.'[3] That is only true, of course, if we believe with Newman that life is for action. There has always been a body of opinion in England that held the opposite view. Action is the last thing they want; but if we want it, it's the men and women of faith who provide it.

The doubters, too, have their advantages and disadvantages. Their main disadvantage is their relentless negativity. Their withering criticality can suppress creativity and all of life's crazy and unpredictable joys. If they get to the top of an institution they ram the cork in the bottle and keep it shut. They resist change. They mistrust life and choose to get through it with the least possible danger. If they have any theology at all it is usually, and often exclusively, a conviction about the centrality of the doctrine of original sin, which is the theological equivalent of Murphy's Law, that if a thing can go wrong it will. Send a bright and enthusiastic curate to work under such a person and you get a recipe for despair and constant conflict. It is one of the paradoxes of the ministry that the life of faith, which is premised upon a wild and unverifiable assumption, should produce so many depressed and unadventurous ministers. It's as though they had used up all their trust getting through the first article of the creed and had no energy left for anything else.

But doubters have certain advantages that benefit the rest of us. They test ideas and some ideas are bad and need to be tested to destruction. They detect phonies and frauds a mile off, and we need to be protected from phonies and frauds. Their best and most enduring contribution to human history is their endless scepticism towards those in power. The powerful are not simply politicians or leaders of institutions. There are the powerful arbiters of intellectual fashion, who tell the rest of us what we may or may not think, or what attitudes we may or may not hold. These inflated and opinionated creatures need to be constantly challenged by sceptics, who refuse to march in step to the beat of the loudest drummer.

Pure trusters and pure doubters probably do not exist. Doubters have to trust something, even if it's only the validity of their own rationality; and trusters have to doubt something, even if it's only the exclusive claims of rationality to apprehend reality. Nevertheless, somewhere along the continuum that stretches between trust and doubt we shall find ourselves. We have our tendencies, our personality profiles, and here, as in everything, it is important to know ourselves. There is something of a vogue in personality testing at the moment. It has become a cottage industry in many Roman Catholic convents that I know, which promote the Myers Briggs personality test. Much of this preoccupation with our own personalities is healthy and useful, though some of it is inevitably narcissistic.

Without using the words in any technical sense, I would like to posit two personality profiles that correspond to the trusting/doubting typology. There is much to be said for doing a personal audit from time to time to know one's biases, one's strengths and weaknesses. A possible profile for the doubter would define such a person as logical, analytical, rational, governed by the head and the reason in apprehending reality. The truster's profile, on the other hand, would be more intuitive and immediate, almost instinctive, disposed to trust the heart and the immediacy of insight and impulse in the apprehension of reality. While accepting that there are no pure types in this typology, we ought to be able to identify our own tendency. We should try to understand why we operate the way we do. We should try to develop compensatory strategies if we are managing our lives incompetently.

We know that doubters are often racked by faith, just as believers are racked by doubt. Doubt in a settled pattern of atheism can be just as disturbing to the unbeliever as doubt in a settled pattern of belief to the believer.

There may even be something in masculine and feminine characteristics (and please note I'm not talking about *male* or *female* characteristics, but about certain human attributes that are conventionally characterized as masculine and feminine, though they can be as easily found in one gender as the other). The feminine type, what Jung would call 'the anima', could be described as receptive, in contrast to the masculine characteristic of assertiveness, the disposition always to challenge. The feminine might be characterized as being more open and trusting towards external influences, while the masculine is often closed against them and defiantly opposed to them. And again there is the contrast between intuition and reason, between a sympathetic immediacy of apprehension and a cooler, more analytical induction of it.

If the tension between faith and doubt is productive of pain and disagreement in the human sphere, in relations between men and women who can see, touch and disagree with one another, it will be obvious that the tension will be wonderfully heightened when we come to that level of discourse we call theology, which seeks to struggle with the very mystery that may or may not lie behind the physical universe. We find exactly the same dynamic at work, though its consequences and conclusions are vaster and less available to human assessment.

76

We find ourselves thrown into a universe that comes without an explanatory leaflet attached. There is no message on the kitchen table, 'Make yourself at home; I'll be back at four o'clock.' This universe suggests both presence and absence. It suggests the absence of a presence that haunts us, and the presence of an absence that puzzles us.

Rational people will go to work on such a universe and produce a rationally justified God, or a rationally justified absence of God. In a mysterious way I find either conclusion chilling. The clinical atheist and the clinical theist, like Molly O'Grady and the officer's lady, are sisters under the skin. Each conclusion is the work of human reason. Conclusive arguments for the existence of God and conclusive arguments against, are just that — conclusive arguments. Empiricists who validate reality by a principle of testable availability dismiss the existence of God as something that is literally beyond our knowing; while inductive theists claim that the rigorous application of the unbiased mind to the mystery of the universe points inevitably to a theistic resolution. Neither of these approaches warms my heart or convinces my will. Each of them conveys the suggestion of an unadmitted agenda, a third element we are not allowed to see, that really clinches the argument for them but not for me. Each of them has a need to control the action, to be in charge, to fix the bets, to remove the unpredictability, to clear up the mystery.

A million miles away from this triumphant rationality is the intuition of the naturally devout, the intrinsic believer somehow born remembering the unutterable

77

mystery. The existence of God for them is not an element in a rational theory of the universe, a conclusion to an argument, or an intellectual category, but a prevailing assurance. 'Two and two only supreme and luminously self-evident beings, myself and my creator', said John Henry Newman. William Temple would have said, 'Amen', at least to the second part of Newman's double claim. William Blake and Francis Thompson wouldn't have bothered to argue, so convinced were they that a ladder was set up between heaven and Charing Cross. Though I am far from sharing their divine composure, I instinctively feel that such intuitive believers have things the right way round. The reality of the divine mystery is assumed until it is proved false; or just assumed as a great act of primordial security and trust. This is what men and women really at home in the world would know in their innermost being and would be in tune with. We are born believing; atheism we have to be taught. Yet we know that the disposition that promotes atheism is important to us; it is, if we can use language in this way, God-given. If God *is*, does God care if we believe or think we don't believe? Paul Tillich developed a useful contrast when he talked about 'the Catholic substance and the Protestant principle', the Catholic substance being the great, enduring given thing upon which human rationality had to work and against which it had to protest. The Catholic substance is the basic and primordial thing without which the Protestant principle could not exist, would have nothing to do. The critical principle is contingent to, dependent upon, the given thing. Is the paradox of atheism and its purifying work found here? Does it raise a necessary protest against believing, not only in the wrong thing but in the right thing for the wrong reason? And the frustration that we feel in grappling with it, might it not owe its elusiveness to this instinctive sense we have that, impressive as it is, it is secondary to the thing it protests against and could not, in fact, exist if the other reality did not first exist. We deny God, because God affirmed us first.

Certainly both passions have to be kept together, which is what Thomas Carlyle was getting at in his great passage about David Hume and Samuel Johnson:

> It is noteworthy that, in our little British Isle, the two grand Antagonisms of Europe should have stood embodied, under their very highest concentration, in two men produced simultaneously among ourselves. Samuel Johnson and David Hume . . . were children of nearly the same year; through life they were spectators of the same Life-movement; often inhabitants of the same city. Greater contrast, in all things, between two great men, could not be . . . .

> They were the two half-men of their time: whoso should combine the intrepid Candour and decisive Clearness of Hume, with the Reverence, the Love and devout Humility of Johnson were the whole man of a new time. Till such whole man arrive for us, and the distracted time admit of such, might the Heavens but bless poor England with half-men worthy to tie the shoe-latchets of these, resembling these even from afar.[4]

What does all this mean? Do we possess specific faculties that put us in touch with the divine mystery, stronger, more developed in some than in others, exaggerated in some, non-existent in others? It is significant that very cerebral, rational people are often emotionally incompetent and bad at relating to others in an ordinary, caring way, unable to break out of their own autistic intellectuality. There are other people who are emotionally undisciplined: like badly tuned shortwave radio sets, they pick up everything on the airwaves, and their lives play like Italian operas. This seems partly to be a function of personality, partly a function of culture. Is it possible that there is an intuitive, spiritual faculty that has been crowded out by the dominant intellectual culture of our time, which has overthrown the softer faculties of wonder and receptivity?

My own theory is that much of this has to do with the lack of silence in our lives, and by lack of silence I don't just mean the prevalence of noise, though noise is clearly a major source of spiritual pollution and psychic disturbance in our time. If there is a mystery that seeks to touch us, we cannot hear its approach in our culture, unlike the Bushman in the Kalahari or the Aborigine in Australia under the vast silence of the night sky. Has the faculty for wonder been atrophied by the critical dynamic of our technological society, with its endless noise, even if the noise is heard only in our heads? It is certainly difficult to find real silence today, yet most of the great religions have come from the desert, not from Manhattan.

Somehow, we must struggle to retain the dialectic

between trust and doubt, between credulity and criticality. The totally credulous or too trusting person becomes a caricature of spiritual obesity, uncritically swallowing something from every cult and craze; while absolute criticality can lead to spiritual anorexia, an inability to receive anything from the mystery that pervades us and so spiritually starves itself to death. The tragedy of today's Church is that it often seems to consist only of theological maximalists and theological minimalists, balloons wrestling with skeletons. Neither seems to me to have understood the precarious security of real trust. They each have a neurotic need for certainty, but the certain no longer need to trust. When God bids us walk across the waters we are not sent inflatable shoes, but there is some instinctive skill that keeps us from sinking. But since it is water we walk on, and not dry land, we can begin to sink if we start thinking in the wrong way about what we are doing. Doubt is the element on which trust walks. It's not always easy to keep our balance, and pride or fear will sink us.

Because there is such an intrinsic connection between faith and doubt, the Church ought to be big enough to contain both sympathetically. This is the kind of theological magnanimity that is important for itself, but it is also important for secondary reasons. Since it is possible to believe and to doubt for the wrong reasons as well as the right ones, and we don't always know the one from the other, we need the constant challenge of the other tendency to keep us honest. This will make life uncomfortable, of course, but the work of our purgation demands it. Growth is painful, but no element in our nature is exempt from the process of sanctification. The Church, unlike the sect, should be as inclusive as possible. It should be big enough to hold Thomas the empiricist, as well as John the mystic, and Peter, who was often baffled and confused. Its heart should be broad and sympathetic enough to hold the whole world, because it was the world for whom Christ died, not a self-congratulatory élite, a truth captured in a fragment of verse I found on a gay friend's bulletin board:

> They drew a circle that shut me out —
> Heretic, rebel, a thing to flout.
> But love and I had the wit to win.
> We drew a circle that took them in.

How the Church in its policies and liturgies might reflect this divine magnanimity is another subject, but it could probably begin in its worship by having more silence and fewer words.

Anyway, the paradox of justification by faith is that it is God's faith in us that ultimately matters and not our faith in God. There is a faith beyond faith, which is deeper than trust in our own trustfulness and is an abandonment to the ultimate graciousness of the universe, even though we have ceased to perceive it or experience it as such. This is the trust beyond trust that says 'yes' even to the night. It is close to the dereliction of Good Friday. The awfulness of the thing may be that absolute trust can only be held in a passionate equilibrium with absolute doubt. Who can bear to be hung upon such a cross? One did. Did he thereby remove the necessity from the rest of us? I don't know. But I *do* know that for some the level of doubt becomes unbearable. If this is the case with them, let them depart. They sin not. Sometimes the departure is gradual, a supervised withdrawal. This is what I think Cupittism is. It's a sort of theological methadone treatment for those who find it difficult to kick the God habit immediately. Dr Cupitt, in his white coat, will take you down gradually, though one day, if you are honest, you are going to have to get off methadone and go it alone. Some brave spirits kick the habit immediately: they do cold turkey. For some, that may be the way to handle excruciating doubt, but it's not the only way. There is also the way of gentleness and waiting. If the night is dark, wait for daybreak. It usually comes.

Notes

1 James Thompson (1834-82).
2 Jane Walmsley, *Brit-Think, Ameri-Think*. Penguin, N.Y. 1987.
3 John Henry Newman, *An Essay in Aid of a Grammar of Assent* (Oxford 1985).
4 Thomas Carlyle, *Essay on Boswell's Life of Johnson*.

Death

One of the great arts of the cinema is the flashback. The cinematic flashback is a case of art reflecting life. It is something we all do. We call to mind, remember faces and incidents from our dear dead past. Another cinematic technique is the flash-forward. Probably because my mother took us to the pictures twice a week during the Second World War, I have been a movie fan all my life. I can remember how, as a boy, I found the techniques of flashback and flashing forward evocative and compelling. I especially loved the technique used in swashbuckling epics to signal a major transition to the future. The hero of the film had been born and abandoned, or, as a child, had seen his parents killed in an outlaw raid, and the camera would shift to a calendar lying on a table; a wind would rise and blow the months and years out of the door until the date was reached at which the action of the film was to be resumed. Even more evocative is the nostalgic use of the flashback at the end of a movie. I can remember the flashback from a film I saw in 1945, when I was eleven years old, though I have not seen the film since, and can remember little about it. It was called *The Sullivans*, or *The Fighting Sullivans*, and it was directed, I've

84

discovered since, by Lloyd Bacon in 1944. It was the story of a large Irish American family of sons, all of whom go off to the Second World War and few of whom come back. The thing that captivated me at the end of the movie was the credit sequence that flashed back to earlier scenes in the lives of the brothers before they had gone off to war. This is a technique used effectively by Michael Cimino in his controversial film of 1978, *The Deerhunter*. At the end of the film the surviving friends go from a funeral to their favourite bar. They sit drinking beer and start singing 'God Bless America'. As the credits play there are flashbacks to the time of pre-Vietnam innocence.

The cinema uses this technique with particular power, because it is a visual medium and much of our remembering is visual, as we play the film of our own past in our minds. Hollywood did not invent this technique, it simply transferred it to film; and it's not just the cinema that plays with this technique. Poetry has always done it. Of British poets, John Betjeman seems to me to be the best at capturing the bittersweet power of remembrance. One of his most evocative poems is 'Old Friends':

The sky widens to Cornwall. A sense of sea
    Hangs in the lichenous branches and still there's
                         light.
The road from its tunnel of blackthorn rises free
    To a final height,

And over the west is glowing a mackerel sky
    Whose opal fleece has faded to purple pink.
In this hour of the late-lit, listening evening, why
    Do my spirits sink?

The tide is high and a sleepy Atlantic sends
    Exploring ripple on ripple down Polzeath shore,
And the gathering dark is full of the thought of
                              friends
    I shall see no more.

Where is Anne Channel who loved this place the
                              best,
    With her tense blue eyes and her shopping-bag
                            falling apart,
And her racy gossip and nineteen-twenty zest,
    And that warmth of heart?

Where's Roland, easing his most unwieldy car
    With its load of golf-clubs, backwards into the lane?
Where Kathleen Stokes with her Sealyhams? There's
                           Doom Bar;
    Bray Hill shows plain;

For this is the turn, and the well-known trees draw
                            near;
    On the road their pattern in moonlight fades and
                            swells;
As the engine stops, from two miles off I hear
    St Minver bells.

What a host of stars in a wideness still and deep;
    What a host of souls, as a motor-bike whines away
And the silver snake of the estuary curls to sleep
    In Daymer Bay.

Are they one with the Celtic saints and the years
                            between?

Can they see the moonlit pools where ribbonweed
drifts?
As I reach our hill, I am part of a sea unseen —
The oppression lifts.[1]

Human beings are rememberers. Our consciousness
involves us in remembering, sometimes inadvertently,
when some trivial incident in the present brings back a
keen memory from the past. It is probably more
accurate to say that we are 'remembrancers': there is
something in us that consciously tries to bring the past
back into focus, to make acts of remembrance. We do
this because we enjoy it, derive pleasure from a past
emotion recalled in tranquillity. But we also do it from
a kind of instinctive piety, from a need to gather up
the fragments of the past that nothing may be lost. It is
said of dogs, though I do not know on what evidence,
that their consciousness is immediate. All the tail-
wagging affection that suggests that they've been
waiting, piningly, at the front door for our return, is
apparently instantaneously generated. Well, that may
not even be true of dogs, but it's certainly far from
being true of humans. We are remembrancers. This is
why exile is such a piercing theme in human history
and the literature that reflects it. Anyone who has
lived abroad for any length of time will know the
weakening influence of such remembrancing, and the
strange alchemy that bathes one's homeland in a
golden glow, the way a cameraman by rubbing
Vaseline on the lens of his camera can subtly alter the
quality of the picture.

We would probably be remembrancers even if we

lived for ever, but it seems to be the presence of death that provokes the keenest remembrance. The living we can revisit, but the dead we can only remember. And we do: sometimes in little glimpses, like the credit flashbacks at the end of a film; sometimes in more elaborate sequences, in which we reconstitute as much about a person as we çan. It is death that makes us look back in sorrow, makes us remembrancers. But it is also death that makes us look forward in dread. It makes us anticipators. I can still remember vividly the moment that death became a personal fact for me. It was during one of the long summers of the Second World War, days of double summertime, when it was light till midnight in the town where I lived in Scotland. There was a war going on and a lot of the men were away, but the real horror of that summer was an outbreak of poliomyelitis among children. There was a panic in the towns in our area. The swimming baths were closed down, because it was thought that the virus was carried in the water. I remember the anxiety of the mothers and my own increasing awareness that we were all at risk. Then it came to our street, to the house opposite, to a boy we knew called Peter, whose father worked on the railway. Peter was 12 when he died, the first death I had registered. I can still remember the grief and the fear in our street:

> From a proud tower in the town,
> Death looked gigantically down

as Edgar Allan Poe described it.

Our consciousness makes us anticipators of our own

dying and the dying of those we love. Death is an abiding part of our consciousness. It is a daily experience, and one of the most solemn duties and privileges of the Church is to help humanity remember the dead and anticipate its own dying. In fact, it has always tried to do this, sometimes badly, sometimes with cruelty, but it has tried. However, there is a particularly mean-spirited strand of Christian history that has sought to trample upon the instinct of remembrance, with unhappy results. In *Geoffrey Madan's Notebooks* there is a wise admonition:

When the Church neglects a duty, a sect springs up:

Anointing of sick:	Christian Science
Prayers for the dead:	Spiritualism
Confession:	Psycho-analysis[2]

In the second item in his list he is recognizing the instinctive human need for formal remembrancing of the beloved dead. When the Church refuses to guide and enable this instinct, it does not thereby disappear, it finds other ways of expressing itself.

Even if they would never use the phrase, most people pray for their own dead. It is true that there have been abuses here, but they have usually been tied to mechanistic and manipulative doctrines of salvation or anxieties over the whereabouts of the dead. There is a natural need to make acts of remembrance of the dead in the context of prayer and worship. It seems pedantic and fussy, as well as profoundly unnatural, to stop praying for people, just because they have died. Their faces, as we have seen,

89

cannot be banished from the screen of our mind; they will appear unbidden, anyway. It is a profound instinct to call them to mind, to bring them with us in our prayer to God, as we did in the days of their living. The broadest streams of Christian tradition have always done this, sometimes elegantly, sometimes crassly. The wisest teachers have known instinctively that it was their privilege to guide human nature in this way. They have understood that one of the purposes of the Church is, through grace, to perfect nature and not denounce it. Christianity, at its best, has baptized human uses and cultures in the name of Christ. Only at its worst has it insisted on cultural emigration from its converts, usually at a great and unnecessary cost.

There is a particularly pedantic type of Protestant mind that would rather ban a good thing that has become distorted than try to reform it, or just live with it. All human uses are mixed, but Christ told us that the truest wisdom lies in letting the tares and the wheat grow together till harvest. Unfortunately, there have been too many Christians who have known better than Christ, who have spent their energies making havoc of the harvest by obsessively pulling at the tares. They have done it in moral theology, with their compulsive need to attack vice rather than try to encourage virtue. And they have done it in ascetical theology, with their arrogant insistence on telling people how they may *not* pray, rather than wisely encouraging them how to. There is a song from the musical *South Pacific*, sung by a Eurasian nurse who remembers the bitter experiences of racial prejudice.

She tells us that children have to be taught to hate. Left to themselves, they would be colour-blind and unprejudiced. Unfortunately, they *are* taught how to hate. There is some naïvety in the claim, but there is also much truth. There is a goodness, as well as a proneness to error and excess, in our natural and instinctive pieties. To be told we may not remember or pray for our dead is as arrogant as being told we may not receive the Eucharist if we slept with our spouse last night.

The most that can be said here is surely the expression of personal preference, accompanied by a possible explanation of it. On a topic as uncertain and elusive as this, there can be no excuse for magisterially determining another's position. It is a melancholy fact, however, that Christians have felt, in this and other matters, that they had a right to dictate the conduct and preferences of others. In the face of the great mystery of death we should operate with enormous reserve and sensitivity. When we speak at all, we should speak only to affirm and console.

Ministry at death remains one of the most privileged and self-evidently useful tasks of the Church. We know from the literature of bereavement how important the right words are on these occasions, and how wounding and yet how common are the wrong words. There are three main elements in this fundamental ministry of grief. The first is a clear and uncompromised acknowledgement of the sorrowful fact of death. This death, and *this death* means every death, is a <u>loss</u> and a <u>wounding</u> to someone. The loss and its attendant agony have to be expressed, found a voice. In the way

91

that public vows at a wedding establish for everyone the *fact* of marriage, so the public declaration of death allows the cruel fact to be accepted, registered, in the heart of the bereaved. Only after that is it possible to turn back to life, however regretfully. This is why there is a peculiar and unceasing pain for those who never retrieve the bodies of their beloved dead for burial or cremation. For them the dying is never concluded by the words said over the body, the words that announce to the mourner, 'The person whom you have loved, you have now lost, and you must acknowledge the loss.' Saying these words on behalf of others, expressing their grief, declaring for them the finality of their loss, is a terrible but honourable privilege to which the Christian minister should attend with sensitivity and with an appropriate seriousness.

The second element in this ancient ministry of death is the act of remembrance, the act that calls to mind the beloved dead. As we have seen, this is a kind of prayer, a kind of plea, but it is not an act with clearly defined boundaries. It is not a bargaining with God, not an exercise in vicarious burden-bearing, though if this were a universe in which we were in any sense able to bear the burdens of the dead, why should we not be allowed to do so? This act of remembrancing is a gathering together of the life in order to affirm and conclude it. Those who would deny us the expression of this piety towards our dead claim too much and too little. They behave as if they knew, beyond any shadow of doubt, the state of the dead or knew that their state was now absolutely decided. Some people have an obsessive fear that our liturgical actions might try to change God's mind. Even if we deny that this is our intention, how can they forget the great and insistent voice in Scripture that constantly calls upon God to relent, to repent, to turn his face favourably upon his children? Apparently, we are allowed to do this on behalf of the living, but, for no very obvious reason, we are forbidden to do it on behalf of the dead. By some method of metaphysical calculation they have determined that God's mind may be changed towards a life, but that, after the moment of death to affect the status of the dead is an adamantine impossibility. I'm not sure that I'm comfortable with the kind of language that suggests God's mind can be changed at all by our devices. But to demarcate the prayer instinct so absolutely strikes me as both cruel and mechanistic. It reflects the mysterious meanness of spirit that frequently characterizes the professionally religious, who behave like fussy, minor bureaucrats, concerned only to frustrate the warm desires and affections of the human heart. The refusal to give Christian burial to a suicide or to allow a suicide to rest in consecrated ground, was the worst example of this mysterious coldness of heart that can afflict spiritual people. Laertes' words to the priest who denied his sister Ophelia proper burial should be stamped on the bottom of every Christian practitioner's licence: 'Churlish priest, a ministering angel shall my sister be when thou liest howling.'[3]

The third element in the liturgy for the dead should be an acknowledgement of the grief and loss of the mourners. This acknowledgement should capture both the uniqueness and the ordinariness of human grieving. Grief is universal, but it is also passionately particular. It is here that the word of faith, or the word of resignation for those without faith, may most appropriately be placed. Care has to be taken to avoid the suggestion that the mourners want the pain to be removed and are seeking a formula from us that will banish it. That is not what the grief-stricken want, nor do they want to hear that their pain will get better. Indeed, they may almost be afraid of the knowledge that, in time, the pain will subside to a dull ache. The pain is all that is left of their loyalty to the dead, and why should they not bear it and glory in the bearing of it? Here, again, finding the words to capture the elusiveness of the state is as difficult as it is important.

There is a specifically Christian hope for the dead, but it is not something that can be verified beyond doubt in this life any more than can the existence of God. Though there is a Christian assurance, a Christian confidence, the proving of these claims will come after death. They are verified eschatologically, finally, not here in the midst of our pilgrimage. But though the full confidence of the specifically Christian hope may not be available to everyone, there is a human wisdom we can help to impart to others as we deal with death and bereavement. We can help people to accept the fact of death and its very necessity. In the universe as we know it, if the living never died the world would become a monstrous place.

To obviate the absolute necessity of death, the reproduction of living things would have had to cease soon after it began. The consequence of this would be the absence of all growth, all evolution of the species. Man, the result of a long evolutionary process, would never have appeared on earth, or, on the assumption that he was 'created' on the first day of the biosphere, would never have evolved to his present state. In a word, we can conceive of the absence of death only in an entirely static universe where a determined number of members of different species would have been created in the beginning and remained constant for the duration. I do not know whether such a universe would have been preferable to our own. But there is no doubt that in an evolutionary universe death is a necessity.[4]

As Ignace Lepp says here, in an evolutionary universe death is a necessity and its necessity is spiritual as well as physical. Birth and death give boundaries to our living, define our experience. Human achievement is mysteriously related to the fact of death. We work while it is yet day, knowing that the night cometh when no one can work. I think it was Paul Tillich who described death as the prelude to revelation. The contemplation of our own finitude brings us to the brink of mystery and stimulates our capacity for revelation. A radical New York rabbi has described death as the messiah, the deliverer, the one who delivers us from the bondage of life. Death is the Church's business.

The AIDS epidemic has brought to it a new poignancy. Death is one of the great wounds we have to bear. As we submit to the questions asked by the young who are dying and absorb the anger they feel, it falls to us to be the arbiters of meaning or to bear the

95

pain of perceived meaninglessness. We should not be hasty to explain, or attempt to explain too much. We must not try too quickly to cap the blazing oil well of the anger of the dying young. Let it burn and let us be scorched by it.

Though all deaths are sad, some deaths are fitting. Helping the aged to die peacefully and their children to mourn is, again, about the harvesting of memories. It is given to us to be the poets, the singers of lives that will soon be forgotten. We must take trouble about it. Our words may be the only public acknowledgement of their lives. It is up to us to stake a claim on their behalf, to announce that they were. It is easy for clergy on funeral duty to lose the sense of the preciousness and importance of each dying, but woe unto us if we ignore the little ones that come unto Christ. We are their remembrancers, there to replay the film of their lives, either in prayer or address. Here, as in all things, great magnanimity and kindness is called for. By our ministry Christ and the Church will be judged. We must struggle against behaving like harassed customs officials at a momentous frontier crossing: rather, we must be the celebrants of their lives and the poets of their sorrow.

This ministry to the dead on behalf of the living and to the living on behalf of the dead, is likely to remain fundamental to the Church's ministry long after many other preoccupations have passed away. It is important, therefore, that we know what our theology of death is. Here, again, we have to face the fact that Scripture does not speak with a single voice, so we must not be too confident about our ability to be precise. For instance, if we were so minded, we might announce that the departed had been taken at death into paradise and were now with the Lord, by basing our theology on St Luke's Gospel:

> One of the criminals who were hanged railed at him, saying, 'Are you not the Christ? Save yourself and us!' But the other rebuked him, saying, 'Do you not fear God, since you are under the same sentence of condemnation? And we indeed justly; for we are receiving the due reward of our deeds; but this man has done nothing wrong.' And he said, 'Jesus, remember me when you come into your kingdom.' And he said to him, 'Truly, I say to you, today you will be with me in Paradise.'
>
> (Luke 23.39-43)

Contrariwise, we could argue that the dead sleep in the Lord till the last trumpet summons them to judgement from all the ends of the earth, by basing ourselves on Paul's magnificent but inconsistent treatment of death in 1 Corinthians 15:

> Lo! I tell you a mystery. We shall not all sleep, but we shall all be changed, in a moment, in the twinkling of an eye, at the last trumpet. For the trumpet will sound, and the dead will be raised imperishable, and we shall be changed. For this perishable nature must put on the imperishable, and this mortal nature must put on immortality. When the perishable puts on the imperishable, and

97

the mortal puts on immortality, then shall come to
pass the saying that is written: 'Death is swallowed
up in victory.'

(1 Cor. 15.51-4)

If we are of a speculative turn of mind and interpret
the story of the raising of Lazarus literally, we are likely
to be puzzled about how it was with him between his
death and his being called forth from the tomb four
days later by Jesus. We are told in John: 'Now when
Jesus came, he found that Lazarus had already been in
the tomb four days' (John 11.17). This story, if we are
inclined to argue from Scripture in this way, might
suggest that the Pauline sleep theory of death is correct,
and that Lazarus was called from the sleep of death
rather than the nearer presence of God, as was the
daughter of Jairus in Mark 5.39, where Jesus asked the
company why they wept because 'The child is not
dead but sleeping'.

And what are we to make of that mysterious theme
in the New Testament that says some of the disciples
would not die before the return of Christ, and
particularly of the rumour that the beloved disciple
would not die, because of the words in John's Gospel:

Jesus said to him, 'If it is my will that he remain until
I come, what is that to you? Follow me!' The saying
spread abroad among the brethren that this disciple
was not to die; yet Jesus did not say to him that he
was not to die, but, 'If it is my will that he remain
until I come, what is that to you?'

(John 21.22-3)

We run into difficulties in interpreting Scripture if we insist on an inner coherence, a harmonic whole, instead of a series of partial and inconsistent insights. There is no systematic theory in the New Testament about the status of the dead, nor should we expect one. The Christian faith is not a prepackaged system, like a computer user's manual that answers all our questions and anticipates many we would never dream of asking. It is a dynamic personal relationship that constantly unfolds with the drama and surprise of any friendship between interesting people. It is important to remember, in particular, that Paul, who is undeniably important in establishing the Christian attitude to death, did not always work out all the implications of his own theories and insights. It has been pointed out, for instance, that Paul himself did not work out all the implications of his great insight in Galatians 3.28: 'There is neither Jew nor Greek, there is neither slave nor free, there is neither male nor female; for you are all one in Christ Jesus.' He carried forward into his practice and theological exposition only the first element of this great trilogy of Jew and Greek, slave and free, male and female. Paul established the place of the Gentiles in Christianity for all time, but it was left to others, at a much later date, to establish the rights of slaves; and it is only in our own time that the rights of females are being established, so that Paul's great trilogy will be finally acknowledged.

Paul, like any busy leader, probably allowed events to dictate his priorities. There are obvious internal inconsistencies in his exposition of the great resurrection hope. For instance, he argues powerfully for the uniqueness, or at least the primacy, of Christ's resurrection. He uses two words in describing the resurrection. He calls it both *aparxe* and *arrabon*.

The word *aparxe* is usually translated 'first fruits'. It refers to the first harvest sheaf reaped, which was offered as a gift of God. The first sheaf is a pledge and promise, the beginning of the harvest. The resurrection of Christ, says Paul, is the first sheaf in the whole harvest of creation. The reconstitution and glorification of the man Jesus Christ is a pledge and promise of the reconstitution and glorification of all things.

> He is the head of the body, the church; he is the beginning, the first-born from the dead, that in everything he might be pre-eminent. For in him all the fulness of God was pleased to dwell, and through him to reconcile to himself all things, whether on earth or in heaven, making peace by the blood of his cross.
>
> (Col. 1.18-20)

The meaning of *aparxe* is best understood by considering another characteristic Pauline word, which he uses almost interchangeably with it, *arrabon*:

> For while we are still in this tent, we sigh with anxiety; not that we would be unclothed, but that we would be further clothed, so that what is mortal may be swallowed up by life. He who has prepared us for this very thing is God, who has given us the Spirit as *a guarantee*.
>
> (2 Cor. 5.4-5)

100

The word the RSV translates as a guarantee is *arrabon*, a commercial term that signifies a pledge, a deposit or first instalment that pays part of the total debt and gives a legal claim. Here is an example from the Old Testament:

> And he said, 'I will send you a kid from the flock.' And she said, 'Will you give me a pledge (*arrabon*), till you send it?' He said, 'What pledge shall I give you?' She replied, 'Your signet and your cord, and your staff that is in your hand.'
>
> (Gen. 38.17-18)

Both *aparxe* and *arrabon* have a future reference. They start a process that runs on to a larger completion. They are terms of hope, pledges for the future.

Paul proclaims the fact that in the resurrection of Jesus Christ God has given us a pledge and promise of the redemption of the whole of creation from change and decay. He has given us a foretaste, a first instalment of his plan for the whole creation.

> For he has made known to us in all wisdom and insight the mystery of his will, according to his purpose which he set forth in Christ as a plan for the fulness of time, to unite all things in him, things in heaven and things on earth.
>
> (Eph. 1.9-10)

Paul argues from the particular fact of Christ's resurrection to the great Christian hope of a transfigured creation. The resurrection message would be easier to deal with if he'd left it at that, but in his great extemporization in 1 Corinthians 15 he begins to argue from the general to the particular, from the alleged fact of a general resurrection back to Christ's resurrection:

> Now if Christ is preached as raised from the dead, how can some of you say that there is no resurrection of the dead? But if there is no resurrection of the dead, then Christ has not been raised; if Christ has not been raised, then our preaching is in vain and your faith is in vain. We are even found to be misrepresenting God, because we testified of God that he raised Christ, whom he did not raise if it is true that the dead are not raised. For if the dead are not raised, then Christ has not been raised. If Christ has not been raised, your faith is futile and you are still in your sins. Then those also who have fallen asleep in Christ have perished.

> (1 Cor. 15.12-18)

Paul slides around a bit in his exposition of the resurrection hope, but there can be little doubt about the central fact that he proclaims. As with salvation, so with resurrection: our hope lies in God alone. Just as we are saved by grace and given our ultimate safety and security freely, through no human effort or achievement, so our destiny beyond death is something that comes freely from the gracious power of God, and not from any undying element in our own character. Paul does not put his trust in an immortal human soul, in some element in the human personality that survives death and escapes from the prison of the body at death into a new sphere of being. But it is difficult to avoid using this kind of language. Indeed, some Christian philosophers, following Plato, would argue for the existence in each of us of an immortal soul. We do not know if such a reality exists, or how we might prove or disprove it, but its existence is certainly not the basis of the Christian hope. Paul is quite clear about this. Our hope is in God alone, in death as in life.

Hope, *elpis*, is the keyword in Paul's understanding of the resurrection. In the Old Testament *elpis* is a general confidence in God's protection and help. God is the hope or confidence of the righteous. In the Greek understanding of *elpis*, hope is the prudent foresight that works with factors that can be controlled, but in the Old Testament hope is precisely focused upon the One who cannot be controlled. Everything in the present is provisional. Hope becomes increasingly hope in the eschatological future:

> O God, our help in ages past,
> Our hope for years to come . . .

as Isaac Watts paraphrased Psalm 90.

The New Testament depends on the Old Testament in its use of *elpis*. Hope is fixed on God. It has three elements: expectation for the future; trust; and the patience of waiting. Hope trusts to the degree that it cannot control the action. Hope cannot count on 'the things that are seen', because everything visible belongs to the world on which no hope can be founded. Christian hope rests on God. It is essential to understand the radical nature of Christian hope. It is not just confidence in the future, though it is certainly that. Paul suggests in his hymn of love in 1 Corinthians 13 that even when the consummation has been

103

achieved, when we will know God as fully as we are known by God, hope will endure: 'Faith, hope, love abide, these three' (1 Cor. 13.13). This is because hope is not based on a human dream but on a confidence that waits for God's gift and, when it is received, does not trust in its own possession of it but in the assurance that God will maintain what God has given. Even in heaven, Christian existence is inconceivable without hope, because hope is the future tense of faith. The biblical conception of hope removes the ground from any security in human nature. Biologically, we are destined to return to dust. Only God can raise that dust to newness of life. Only God can transform our finitude and rescue us from death. But even at the consummation, at the resurrection of the dead, our new life will remain an eternal gift of God in Christ. In other words, Christian hope is an abiding trust in the God who called us out of nothing into life and who will call us again to life out of the second nothing of death. We have no security in ourselves, no false hopes, no naive longings. Our only ground of hope is the God who raised Jesus Christ from the dead as 'the first-fruits of them that slept'.

Paul's teaching on hope is at one with his conception of the radical nature of grace. In our dealings with God everything is grace, everything is gift. Our expectation of eternal life is rooted in God alone. It does not reside in our own undying essence. Our expectations lie in the promise of a reliable God who has already, in Christ, set the action of our resurrection in motion. Christ's resurrection is the assurance and the beginning of our resurrection — it is both *arrabon* and *aparxe*, a pledge and a beginning. In the language of the cinema, it is a preview, a trailer, of what's coming next, a future presentation.

We are indeed dust and to dust we shall return; but as Augustine has told us: 'We have begun to be some great thing. We were once nothing, but we are something. We had said, "Remember that we are dust"; but out of the dust he made man, and to dust he gave life, and in Christ he hath brought this dust to the kingdom of heaven.'

Death reminds us of the weakness and the glory of humanity. The universe defeats us, brings us to dissolution, reminds us that we are but dust. But we are glorious dust, troubled dust, dust that challenges the universe. Death defeats us, but doesn't know it. But we defeat death and the universe over which it rules, by knowing it, acknowledging it, looking it in the face. Pascal captured the paradox like this:

> Man is only a reed, the weakest thing in nature — but a thinking reed. It does not take the universe in arms to crush him; a vapour, a drop of water, is enough to kill him. But, though the universe should crush him, man would still be nobler than his destroyer, because he knows that he is dying, that the universe has the advantage of him; the universe knows nothing of this.[5]

'We have begun to be some great thing', said Augustine. We know ourselves to be and that knowing of our weakness is the beginning of our greatness. It is the prelude to revelation, the apprehension of our nature as a reality that generates a question about itself it cannot answer, yet cannot abandon. 'The troubles of our proud and angry dust are from eternity and will not fail,' said Housman.[6] We have either created eternity to trouble our own hearts with longing or have been created by it. There is our choice. And death brings us to it again and again.

The community of faith never quite knows whether it has chosen or been chosen by God, but it finds its own life interpreted by the narrative of faith. Again and again it walks disconsolately to Emmaus and finds Another walking with it, interpreting its pain and rekindling its hope. It is the exasperating nature of hope to be self-evidencing to the believing heart, but non-negotiable as an exchange commodity in the currency of human discourse. This is probably because it is never possessed, never owned, but only guaranteed; and we either trust the guarantee or we don't. Christ Jesus, in his dying and rising in the proclamation of the Church, is the guarantee, the pledge of our own beginning. But lest we should boast of our possessing him and use him to justify ourselves, we are brought by our sinfulness to rely on his grace alone, and we are brought by our dyingness to hope in his grace alone. That is always the way it is: Christ is encountered, never explained. We can tell what has happened to us on our journey, but we can never transfer the experience to someone else's account and we do not have to try. But as the community of faith shares its story on the way, struggling to understand it, the one who has gone before us all into death draws near and goes with us, and our failed explanations finally become prayer and the connection occurs. It is always different but it is always the same. Luke got it as nearly right as it ever gets: 'Then they told what had happened on the road, and how he was known to them in the breaking of the bread' (Luke 24.35).

Notes

1 John Betjeman, *High and Low* (John Murray 1966), pp. 11, 12.
2 *Geoffrey Madan's Notebooks* (Oxford 1985), p. 3.
3 *Hamlet*, V.i.260.
4 Ignace Lepp, *Death and its Mysteries* (Burns & Oates 1969), pp. 7, 8.
5 Blaise Pascal, *Pensées*.
6 A. E. Housman, 'The Chestnut Casts His Flambeaux', *Poetry and Prose*, Hutchinson 1971.

Epilogue

In the first sentence of this book I asked if the Christian message was good news for sinners. The question was an obvious echo of the foundational claim of Christianity that it has a gospel for the world. The word gospel comes from the old English word *godspel*, meaning good news, a translation of the Greek word *euaggelion*. A pre-Christian use of the word tells us that the Emperor Augustus' birthday is 'for the world, the beginning of things which owing to him are glad tidings', an inscription which is echoed in the announcement of the angels to the shepherds in the fields above Bethlehem that they brought good tidings of great joy for all people. The glad announcement of the birth of a baby is a classic example of good news. Good news, gospel, is something we can't help sharing, something we can't keep to ourselves. It bubbles out of us almost against our will. In illustrating this characteristic of gospel, Leslie Weatherhead said that good news was something that could be shouted across the street to a friend. It is still a good test: 'The hostages are home!' 'Mary's had a baby!' 'The X-ray is clear!' 'I got the job!' The background to these gospel messages shouted across the street at delighted friends is a background of anxiety and fear. This is a world in which hostages are taken, a world in which giving birth to a child is risky. It's a world in which people die of cancer, a world where people can't find jobs. So these tidings shared irresistibly with our friends are indeed good news, gospel. A minute's reflection tells us why they are glad tidings.

What is the background to the Christian good news? What is the context in which the Christian message comes as glad tidings to the people of the world? Gospel is always something personal. It's a piece of good news that we have to share and the best way to answer the question I've just put is to tell someone's story, not offer an abstract theological exposition. The best way to understand the meaning of Christianity's claim that it has a gospel for all is to reflect on the life of Simon Peter the apostle. Next to our Lord himself and St Paul, we know more about him than any other character in the New Testament, and what we know is profoundly instructive. We know that Peter enthusiastically followed Christ. We know that he promised, with great passion, to be faithful to him until death. And we know that he deserted him in his moment of need and denied him vehemently after his arrest. Peter's story is a very human story. On all sorts of levels people can identify with it. It captures the human experience of failure to live up to our ideals. To have no ideals may be sad, but it brings with it no sense of failure. To have ideals and never fail them would be a happy state, but to have ideals and fail them is bad news. Failure to live up to our own values is the source of the keenest misery known to human nature. We can see this human dilemma on various levels. In our over indulgent society it has taken on a brutally physical aspect, as people struggle to lose weight, to give up smoking, or to discipline their sexual desires. We can all pose to ourselves ideals of physical beauty, health and a proper restraint in our relationships, but conforming the reality of our nature to our ideals is proverbially difficult. When we move from the realm of physical well-being to mental and moral well-being the struggle becomes even keener: disciplining our tongue, restraining our temper, behaving kindly, even towards our nearest and dearest, can all be incredibly difficult ideals to live up to. So Peter's experience of personal failure is universal, though it was his old opponent Paul of Tarsus who found the words to express it. In the letter to the Romans Paul wrestles with his own nature and states the human dilemma for us all:

> I do not understand my own actions. For I do not do what I want, but I do the very thing I hate. I can will what is right, but I cannot do it. For I do not do the good I want, but the evil I do not want is what I do.
> (Rom. 7.15, 19)

The human tragedy is that we naturally pose ideals for ourselves; we respond almost instinctively to spiritual and moral values at the level of the mind or the heart; but at the level of the will, the executive level, we find that we have a power shortage. We have ideals but we fail them. We long for peace but we plunge ourselves into war. We long for human flourishing but we disfigure the world with our neglect and exploitation of one another. We long for every child to be nurtured in a happy family, but we know that actual families are often miniature war zones that damage children for life.

This disproportion between our moral and spiritual ideals and our actual performance is covered in the Christian tradition by the little word *sin*, and we mean sin in the singular. We don't mean specific sins, such as gluttony, murder or neglect. These, indeed, are the symptoms of human sin but they are not themselves the disease, which is why moralistic preachers who rant against specific human failings are usually beside the point. They attack the symptom when they should be helping people to understand the disease. One of the most common New Testament words for sin has an extremely suggestive history. It is an archery term that means aiming at the target and missing. That captures the human experience well. Our tragedy, our human dilemma, is not that we are uninterested in hitting the target. We are very interested in our ideals, our aims, our objectives. We constantly aim at them, but we miss them time and again. Like St Peter, our deepest sorrow is that we have ideals, genuinely believe in them, but we fail them. Peter's story is the human story.

The most heartbreaking incident in Peter's story is found in Luke's Gospel, just after they have seized Jesus and led him away to the High Priest's house:

> . . . Peter followed at a distance. They lit a fire in the middle of the courtyard and sat round it, and Peter sat among them. A serving-maid who saw him sitting in the firelight stared at him and said, 'This man was with him too.' But he denied it: 'I do not know him,'

111

he said. A little later a man noticed him and said, 'You also are one of them.' But Peter said to him, 'No, I am not.' About an hour passed and someone else spoke more strongly still: 'Of course he was with him. He must have been; he is a Galilean.' But Peter said, 'I do not know what you are talking about.' At that moment, while he was still speaking, a cock crowed; and the Lord turned and looked at Peter. Peter remembered the Lord's words, 'Tonight before the cock crows you will deny me three times.' And he went outside, and wept bitterly.

(Luke 22.54-62)

The devastating thing about Peter's denial is that he was an idealist who genuinely loved the man he denied. Peter was no cynic for whom a betrayal of another was a casual, everyday matter. He was deeply committed to Jesus and meant what he had said only a few hours before the incident in the courtyard: 'Lord, I am ready to go with you to prison and to death.' Peter was a divided man. This was his tragedy. The good that he would he did not, the evil that he sought to avoid he fell into. The tears that he wept, however, were not simply tears of remorse or even repentance. Remorse is a kind of self-reproach, we feel we have let ourselves down. Repentance is deeper. When we repent, we acknowledge that we have let others down. Peter, we can be certain, felt both remorse and repentance, but his tears probably had an even deeper root. Luke tells us that after Peter's third denial the Lord turned and looked at him and Peter remembered how he had said to him, 'Before the cock crows today you will deny me three times.' What probably devastated Peter was the strength of the pity in that look. It was a look not of reproach, but of compassion. Jesus knew the human heart, he knew the depths of agony, self-hatred and sorrow into which Peter was plunging. Peter was not a bad man. A thoroughly bad man sheds no tears. Peter was a divided man, a flawed man, a man who couldn't live up to his own ideals.

So far the story is hardly a cheering one. It's the all-too-common story of a prominent citizen caught out in a public failure. We can almost see the screaming tabloids of Jerusalem blazoning Peter's shame for all to read. If this were a purely and characteristically human story, Peter would spend the rest of his life as a professional failure pathetically trying to justify himself. During the awful McCarthy witch-hunts of alleged communists in the film industry in the USA during the 1950s many people betrayed their friends to avoid being blacklisted themselves. In the 1980s I saw one of these betrayers being interviewed on television. He was a big man, a famous film star, but his face contorted with shame and torment as he recalled how he had betrayed his best friends in order that he might himself continue to work and how they would no longer speak to him. He kept saying, 'It's very hard, it's very hard'; and he was clearly haunted by the memory and the consequences of his own treason. Peter's story was very different. There is no account in the New Testament of the risen Jesus accusing him or even saying, 'I told you so'. Indeed, the nearest we come to any reflection on the incident is in the final chapter of John's Gospel, where Peter is asked three times if he loves Jesus. Each vehement protestation of love must have set up an echo in his mind of those equally vehement denials in the courtyard only days before. The significant thing is that Jesus does not refer to the failure; he fastens on the ideal. He does not condemn the denial; he seeks for the avowal of love. True to his own wise knowledge of the human heart, he did not seek to pull up Peter's sins but to encourage the growth of his love. Peter's story encapsulates the pure essence of the Christian message, which is that we are accepted by God even at the moment of our deepest betrayals.

The revolutionary element in the Christian movement, so revolutionary that organized Christianity has found it almost impossible to live with, is the doctrine of the forgiveness of sins. By definition, forgiveness is about something given back. We cannot take back our denials, cannot undo the wrongs we have too clearly done. They have to be *given* back to us and this is what divine forgiveness means. Again and again God gives back the sins I have committed, and in my divided state this is what I need. In my insecurity and self-hatred I'll defend myself bitterly against your accusations, but if you love me in my sin my heart will break and my love will reach out to your love and I may even grow through my shame into goodness. And that is how God responds to me. That is the good news, the hidden secret of God that lies beneath the harshness of much contemporary Christianity. And again it is best captured by St Paul who tells us in the letter to the Romans:

> While we were yet helpless, at the right time Christ died for the ungodly. Why, one will hardly die for a righteous man — though perhaps for a good man one will dare even to die. But God shows his love for us in that while we were yet sinners Christ died for us.
>
> (Rom. 5.6-8)

As we know ourselves to be today, in all that we condemn in ourselves, God loves us. Frère Roger, in pleading this gospel of absolute grace and unconditional love before thousands of young people from all over the world who come to Taizé each summer, is fond of quoting from the Letter of John: 'If our hearts condemn us God is greater than our hearts' (1 John 3.20). That is the good news. When men and women fully receive it into their hearts and believe it they can't help sharing it, it bursts out of them. One of the ways they share it is by their graciousness towards other sinners. They bless; they do not condemn.

But we don't leave it there, of course. God goes on forgiving us till seventy times seven. God will go on forgiving us as long as we need it. But God also has ambitions for us. Our happiness is God's joy and our happiness only comes when our ideals coincide with our actions, but that usually takes a while. Anyway, that's the *second* part of the story.